THE HISTORY OF THE HAT

THE HISTORY OF THE HAT

By
MICHAEL HARRISON

Line Drawings by VERNET
from contemporary sources

My hat to a half-pence,
Pompey prouues the best
Worthie —
Loues Labours Lost

LONDON: HERBERT JENKINS

First published by
Herbert Jenkins Ltd
3 Duke of York Street
*London, S.W.*1

1960

MADE AND PRINTED IN GREAT BRITAIN BY
WILLIAM CLOWES AND SONS, LIMITED, LONDON AND BECCLES

CONTENTS

ACKNOWLEDGMENTS

THE full acknowledgment, by any writer, of the help that he has received from others in the completing of his book is always a task at once willingly undertaken, morally imperative—and, practically, almost impossible.

To answer, *completely*, the question: "Who helped you?" is as difficult (well-nigh impossible) as to answer the question: "Who educated you?"

One may list one's authorities: but the stray scrap of information goes in, too. I have just picked up a piece of paper—an old envelope—and I find there a note scribbled down as I looked in the window of a print-seller's in Cecil-court. What I wrote down has gone into my book—and there are dozens of such items, as accidentally gathered, as hastily written down, and as gratefully used. Shall I list these among my "authorities"? Must I—can I?—acknowledge them all?

I cannot. At the risk of seeming ungracious or ungrateful to some of those to whom I have owed a piece of information, I can but single out a few—a few books, a few persons—of all those to whom I am indebted. At the end of this volume, under "Source Material," I have listed many books, but only those which have a direct bearing upon the subject of Hats in particular or Costume generally. Yet, to Mr Cyril Pearl's fascinating *The Girl with the Swansdown Seat*, I am indebted for the first full account of all that Fashion owed to the bewitching Skittles. I gratefully acknowledge my debt to Mr Pearl—but I leave his book out of my list of "authorities," since, to include every book or journal to which I have gone for information would be to make the list inexcusably long.

For instance, I owe much to the periodical journals, such as the invaluable *Illustrated London News*, *The Queen* (soon to celebrate its first centenary), *Punch*, and such now discontinued but still, fortunately, available publications as

The Gentleman's Magazine. The files of such old-established newspapers as *The Times, The Daily Telegraph, The Observer, The Sunday Times,* and so on, have had necessarily to be consulted, and have yielded much of value.

However, to single out a few persons to whom I owe particular thanks, I would like to mention Mr John Christie-Miller, Master of the Worshipful Company of Feltmakers, 1956–1957, whose family have been connected with hat-making for four centuries, and who placed his own records at my disposal; Mr J. M. McNulty, Secretary of the British Felt Hat Manufacturers Federation, who contributed the information on felt-hat-making incorporated in this present volume; the Directors of Messrs G. A. Dunn & Co. Ltd, the nationally-known hatters; the Directors of G. W. Scott & Sons Ltd, makers of bearskins for the Guards, and a firm which will, next year, celebrate its tercentenary as London hatters; Mr R. Brown, Librarian of the City of Westminster Public Library, Buckingham Palace-road, and his ever-helpful staff, and all the other Librarians of London; to Mr G. Hallows, for calling my attention to the origin of the "Hat Trick"; to Mr Brian Winston, for information on Jewish ritual headwear; and to my wife, for advice and practical assistance.

THE HISTORY OF THE HAT

Chapter One

HATS—GENERALLY

I F the history of the Hat be nothing like as long as the history of Man, be sure, however, that the Hat is of immeasurable antiquity, and its wearing among the earliest of Man's social institutions.

Yet, archaeological discovery reveals nothing like a "basic hat," any more than scientific philology reveals the patterns of a "basic speech."

And so we can say of the hats of ancient Sumer, exactly what we may say of the speech of ancient Sumer, that "behind these forms lies a long history of development."

A few hours before I began this book, I saw a youth in the Strand wearing what is advertised in a Strand shop as "the new Robin Hood"—a conical-crowned hat with the brim turned up at the back and sides, to press tightly against the crown; the front of the brim being pulled down to form a sort of fore-peak or visor.

Conscious revival: the "Robin Hood"

We know what inspired the designer to introduce this type of headgear for our less conservative youth; and we know, too, what impelled him to call it "the Robin Hood." It is obvious that the designer found his inspiration in a recent television serial.

But, in fact, the history of this particular hat-shape goes a long way back beyond the Late Middle Ages, at which date the romancers like to set that de-divinified minor deity, "Robin Hood."

The "Robin Hood" is, in truth, a hat-form commonly encountered in Greek vase-paintings, especially of the 6th century B.C.

In that archaic period of Hellenic art, the Hero Perseus is often shown as wearing a "Robin Hood," and it is only much later that we encounter him wearing what we had better call his "more classical" type of headgear: the steel helmet of the

Greek, man's, c. 490 B.C.

Round, brimless

Round, brimless

Pork-pie or pill-box

Pork-pie or pill-box

pattern issued to British troops during the two World Wars—winged for Perseus.

A disillusioned antique-dealer, discussing with me the sad showing that modern furniture made in contrast with the old, had this to say:

"There are only certain basic forms you *can* use—and the oldtime designers, from Marot and Buhl, to Hepplewhite and Sheraton, used every one of them. What chance has a modern designer got, anyway . . . ?"

Just so with the hat: here, too, there are basic shapes, and only a handful of them, all told.

There are the brimless hats: crown-fitting (*skull-cap, Basque beret*); low-crowned (*smoking-cap, "pill-box"*); and high-crowned (*clown, magician*). There are the brimmed hats: small-brimmed (*Lock bowler*); medium-wide-brimmed (*boater*); and wide-brimmed (*Spanish caballero*).

We may subdivide each of the brimmed types into flat-brim or curly-brim; and a further subdivision is possible by making the brim dip at some point or other. Pull the brim down in front, and you have the "snap brim felt" (to use the hatters' trade-jargon); pull it down at the back, and you have the style much favoured of mid-Victorian sailors, British, American or French.

Turn the brim up at the side, and you have a style equally favoured of the London night street-cleaner or the Australian Expeditionary Force.

Cowboy-hats are wide-brimmed, and are generally turned up, rather than curled; but in their purposely tattered condition (at least, as shown on the cinema-screen), they hint at a very old custom: that of *dagging*, or the incorporation into the design of marks of imaginary wear-and-tear.

A London hatter of the more "popular" kind sells hats whose crowns have been moulded to suggest that the fore part of the crown has been pinched by a wearer's three-digited grip. If it seem unduly fanciful to suggest that this production of a brand-new "already worn" model must find its logical development in the production of a Petersham hat-riband dyed to resemble head-grease staining, may I point out the curious recurrent male fashion of the Deplorable Old Hat, to be worn with the most elegant suits ?

But assuming that there are only six basic hat-shapes; three brimmed, and three unbrimmed; the variations possible on these six basic themes, either singly or in combination, are many indeed.

We have not yet considered the infinite variations that human ingenuity and human waywardness can give to the stocking cap alone: a type which has not been mentioned, for its wonderful manipulation can put it equally into the brimmed or the unbrimmed class.

Round, small-brimmed

Purists may take me up on the use of that phrase, "stocking cap," when used in relation to the hood-with-liripipe which was *the* mediaeval hat-form. I am well aware that the hood was made of cloth; wool or linen or silk (depending upon one's social station and the money to maintain that station); but it is easier to refer to the liripiped hood as a "stocking cap," because, when it was carried over (without the liripipe) into post-mediaeval times, it was knitted, and not any longer constructed out of whole cloth.

The repeat-pattern in human impulse showed strikingly when the mediaeval gorgeted hood was reintroduced, as an article of military clothing, under the name of Balaclava. Just as the more enterprising of our mediaeval ancestors wore their hoods in any way but the "proper" way, so that almost all the forms of the late mediaeval hat originated in odd ways of wearing the hood, so did our modern soldiers adopt any way of wearing the Balaclava but the "correct" one, i.e., covering head and neck. Such advantages as the "correct" wearing of the Balaclava might offer were held to be as nothing against the advantages offered by a man's expressing his individuality in the highly personal way in which he wore his Balaclava.

Flat-topped, large, flat-brimmed

Personality and hat-fashions are closely connected; so much so that not only will a certain way of wearing a hat attract the name of a real or fictional character (e.g., Rubens, Vandyke, Stanley, John Drew, Anthony Eden; Dolly Varden, Trilby,

Fedora), but even a completely imaginary one, such as "Billy Coke" or "William Bowler."

Man long ago devised a method of taking needed shade with him—and invented the hat, and we may assume that the first hats ever devised by Man consisted either in animal-skin or the leaf of a tree.

The Mexican sombrero

With regard to the latter, the hat made of leaf or stalk or pith is still with us; so much so that two trees, *Thrynax argentea* and *Copernicia cerifera* both bear the name, "hat-palm" or "chip hat-palm," as their leaves are used in hat-making.

There is also an East Indian plant, *Aeschynomene aspera*, whose very tough pith is made into hats. It is commonly known as the "hat-plant."

With regard to the animal-skin cap—the type to the making of which Robinson Crusoe instinctively turned when he found himself hatless in San Juan Fernandez—it is probable that early man knew this in two forms: for both seem to have left traditions which have survived to the present.

The two types oddly conform to our modern distinction between the "hard hat" and the "soft hat"; the "soft hat" being represented, among primitive man, by a cap made of the skin—tanned or untanned—and the "hard hat" by the fur-covered skull of an animal, worn both as protection from the weather and protection from the neighbour's flint-axe.

Animals' skins are still used; but their antiquity is attested by the predilection that military men have not only for animal skins as headwear but for animal-masks, in metal, as part of the regimental headwear's decoration. The origin of the helmet in the animal's skull need not be sought hypothetically in the long tradition of animal-shaped helmets—Scythian, Scandinavian, Greek—but actually in the heads themselves, worn by the Greeks and Romans with the so-called "ritual" armour: a tradition which was perpetuated in heroic sculpture, as far into modern times as the beginning of the 18th century.

Greek helmet, c. 490 B.C.

Early man, with his animistic and anthropomorphic concept of Nature, would have found it impossible to wear either the leaf of a plant or the skin of an animal in what we may call a "utilitarian" frame of mind. To "wear" something, among primitive peoples, is to "possess" it, and having taken away, from plant or animal, its life, bestowed, in the view of primitive man, that ravished life upon the taker. To the owner of leaf or skin would come the *mana*—the subtle essence of being and strength-in-being—which formerly had been the possession of plant or animal.

Garlic, to use, is a strong-tasting herb; though, to the Spaniards, it is a sovereign guard against rheumatism, as well as a flavouring for stews and salads. But the name reveals what it was to our Teutonic ancestors: *gar-leac*—sword-plant. The plant whose power it was specifically to heal wounds caused by the sword.

Eat the garlic, and you acquire the plant's magical power.

Wear the leaf of a tree, and you acquire the shade that the tree *makes*.

Wear the skull of a bull or lion or tiger (after having eaten the brains scooped out of the hot skull), and, magically, you acquire the strength and ferocity of the animal that you have conquered, either by force or cunning.

The distinction, then, noted very early in the history of the hat, between "utilitarian-decorative" and "ritual" headwear is a distinction possible only at a comparatively late period in man's own history. In the beginning of the hat-wearing period, all headwear must necessarily have had something of the "ritual" aspect in their inventing and wearing. It is only as we come out of barbarism into civilization that we find men making the distinction between what was worn on the head for protection against the weather and what was worn as protection against the Gods.

When the Etruscans captured Latium, they did not impose their language on the Latins and Sabines whom they conquered; though they gave names not only to many a noble Roman family, and to many of Rome's hills, but to the Eternal City itself. "Rome" is Etruscan, and so are the names of the City's legendary founders, Romulus and Remus.

Eventually, the Etruscans who stayed in Rome merged with the Latin population; the others, expelled, went back to

Etruscan cap, man's, c. 500 B.C.

Etruscan cap, man's, c. 530 B.C.

Atef *crown of Lower Egypt*

Pshemt *crown of Upper Egypt*

Tuscany, to await their gradual absorption into an ever-expanding Roman state.

Now the Etruscans had a distinctive head-dress: a somewhat "beehive shaped" hat, with a veil encircling it tightly at its lowest edge.

This hat continued to be worn in Tuscany, especially by the nobility, until the end of the 15th century, but in Rome its use was discontinued, *save as the traditional headwear of the Roman priesthood.*

When Constantine made Christianity the State religion, and Christianity took over the organization of the Roman State religion, this ritualized Etruscan head-dress had not yet ended its long ritual life.

It lasted, indeed, until the year 1806, in which year the Emperor Napoleon I decreed the extinction of the Venetian Republic.

For the Etruscan hat, adopted by the Roman priesthood, went—still in its ritual significance—north-west, to Venice; to become the "crown" of the Doge of the Most Serene Republic.

It is perhaps a little far-fetched to connect the distinctive shape of the early Etruscan hat with the distinctively beehive-shaped Mycenean tombs; but it is surely reasonable to connect the adoption of this proscribed "pagan" headgear by the head of the Venetian state with the memorably insolent reply that a Pope got from the Venetian Senate: *Non sumus Christiani, sed Veneziani!*—"We aren't Christians—we're *Venetians*!"

In an earlier age, the Middle Asian shape of the White Crown of Upper Egypt seems to hint that Upper Egypt was conquered by the Egyptians, not as an independent people but as forced levies for Invaders who had already conquered Lower Egypt. It should be noted that the distinctive and unusual shape of the Red Crown of Lower Egypt bears a really striking resemblance to the typical Scythian helmet, with its back rising in a single, high horn.

Another origin of ritual head-dress is to be found in the wearing, as a head-dress, of a divine symbol. The so-called "Moon Disk," always placed over representations of the goddess Isis, is, in fact, a highly conventionalized plan of the bicornute uterus. Priestesses of Isis wore a lightweight version of this symbol of the Great Mother; and, after a male priesthood of Isis had been established, the priests did, too.

It is significant that the mitre of the Jewish High Priest, in the period after the Egyptian captivity, should resemble so closely the "crown of Isis," with the "moon" missing. The mitre of bishops of the Roman and Anglican Churches is simply the ancient Jewish High Priest's "mitre"—the *mishnepheth* or *shaniph*—turned horizontally through an angle of 90 degrees. "Aesthetic" considerations, themselves based on hardly recognized but deep-rooted religio-racial prejudices, have been at work altering the "traditional" shape of the bishops' mitre; making it taller, reducing the inward curve of the points and bringing the flattened points closer together— and generally tending to obscure the direct connection between the present-day mitre and its original (if, indeed, even the "crown of Isis" was the original). But the connection is apparent if we look at a mediaeval mitre; such, for instance, as the mitre reputed to have belonged to Thomas à Becket, Archbishop of Canterbury, and now on view at the Victoria and Albert Museum.

It is interesting to see that the papal tiara has been modified in quite a different direction: to bring its shape more into line with that of the mitre; that is to say, as seen from the front, since the characteristic "bicornute" pattern is missing from the single-pointed papal tiara. The now familiar "leaf-shaped" outline of the tiara dates only from the late Middle Ages: before that time, as may be seen in the many representations of early and mid-mediaeval Popes, the tiara was not only a perfectly regular cone—the straight-sided "dunce's" or "magician's" cap—but is quite often shown as banded with only two crowns, and not the now standard three.

Chapter Two

THE CAP

The Emperor Maximinian, A.D. *286–305*

W

HAT now, did the Anglo-Saxons wear in the way of hats or caps? They were first-rate craftsmen, but they were poor draughtsmen; and men were represented (perhaps for reasons of taboo) in a highly conventionalized fashion. Fortunately, we have two pieces of evidence, not only to show us what at least one of their forms of headgear looked like, but to assure us that, though many men went bareheaded—as the majority of the Latins did—they did wear caps.

The first piece of evidence is philological; the second archaeological.

The late Latin word, *cappa*, which was used to translate the Greek word, *κάππα*, a cap or hat, is the origin of two English words, *cap* and *cope*. (Through the French, we have other derivatives of *cappa*: *cape* and *chapel*.)

Cap, today, and in Anglo-Saxon times, means a head-covering. *Cope*, means a cape reserved for ecclesiastical use.

Now late Latin had a variant spelling of *cappa*—*capa*; and this variation was used by the various Romance languages to distinguish between the two meanings of the word: *hat* or *cape* (*cope*).

How *cappa* came eventually to mean a cape or cope is simple to understand. Originally, the word *cappa*—or *capa*—was applied, not only to a cap, but to the hood attached to a cloak. From this point, there was a transfer of meaning to a cloak having such a hood; and the meaning was then restricted to a special sort of cape: a priest's "cope."

But, Murray observes, "the evidence of Old English is important, since it points to two distinct Latin types, viz. *cappa* (which gave *cæppe*, *cappe*, cap) and *capa*, which gave *cape*, cope; the latter is also witnessed by Icelandic *kapa*, 'cowled cloak, cloak with a hood.'"

18

"It looks," Murray continues, "as if *cappa*, the living Romanic form, was first adopted in England (say from Italy) in the 7th century, and gave *cæppe*, and that, at a later time, *capa*, so common in mediaeval Latin, was introduced especially for the ecclesiastical dress. The latter is not actually evidenced in Old English, but it occurs in Layamon, and was in the language early enough to undergo the phonetic change of Old English *a* into Middle English *o*." (*A New English Dictionary on Historical Principles* by James A. H. Murray.)

The evidence, then, shows that the English, somewhere about the time of Augustine's visit, adopted a foreign word for a normal article of clothing, and one, moreover, having only a secular significance.

Now, we know that the Anglo-Saxons wore some sort of headgear besides their horned helmets and the veils of the women; and, in fact, the existence of so ancient a word as *hat* (A.S. *hæt*: with cognates in all the Teutonic languages) proves it. Why, then, did they adopt a foreign word for a head-covering?

The answer must be that the word, *cap*, was adopted to describe either a novel form of head-covering or a novel way of wearing a head-covering of a traditional type.

"Phrygian" bonnet, Anglo-Saxon, 10th cent.

When a people adopts a foreign word, it is because there is no word in its standard vocabulary to describe a new thing, or a new way of looking at old things.

Such words as *cocoa, chocolate, tobacco, zero, potato, syrup,* were adopted into our language because we had no existing words for the things or ideas that they represented.

The word, *cap*, must, then, have been adopted because it was necessary to describe a form of headwear hitherto unknown to the Anglo-Saxons.

Turn now to the archaeological evidence. The bogs of Jutland have a remarkable preservative power; and when, probably in about the 2nd century of our era, a ritual beheading was suffered by a chieftain, in accordance with established tribal law, his hatted head, thrown into the bog of Tollund, was preserved from corruption to this day. It is from Denmark that the only complete and perfectly preserved costumes of the Ancient World have come, and it is almost miraculous that we can, through the accident of long preservation, actually handle these garments of two thousand years ago: woven, knitted, made of stitched leather—marvel at the fact that the "cricketing trousers" of today, with their belt slotted through loops at the waist, were anticipated by the Danes of only a little after Christ's time.

Greek, man's, c. 480 B.C.

The Tollund man's hat may be taken as representative of at least one type worn by our Anglo-Saxon ancestors. It is of leather, cut in one piece, and folded, with a single seam, to form a "blunt-conical" shape. It is not stitched, but laced with a leather thong; the seam running vertically up from above the right ear. The simplicity of this hat takes nothing away, by its almost primitive plainness, from the noble austerity of the sacrificed chieftain's face. With its thin, high-bridged nose, the face belongs to a racial type impossible to classify as savage; and that hawk-nose, thin lips and massive brow (yet slender templed) may hint at a reason why Teutonic is a language whose *ablaut* system is matched by that of the Semitic tongues.

Burial in an oak coffin is another way of preserving body and clothes almost indefinitely; and to this mode of preservation—accidental though it was—we owe another hat from Denmark's Bronze Age. This is a tall, conical-crowned hat, of material woven from sheep's wool in a twill-weave, and was made in two parts—crown and brim: the two parts being sewn together with a needle. This example was found in a coffin at Borum Aeshøj; and a coffin at Trindhøj yielded a particularly interesting find: a round cap of cloth woven (as was the cloak which accompanied it) with a short pile: the earliest example yet found of "artificial fur."

The resemblance of the Tollund Man's cap to the classic "Phrygian cap" of antiquity is so striking that we may say that here we have a type of cap which is "basic" throughout the Near Eastern and Western world. The graves at Borum Aeshøj, Trindhøj, Muldbjerg, Egtved, Skrydstrup and Guldhøj have yielded articles—notably a folding-chair from Guldhøj of Egyptian design, and a woven shawl from Trindhøj with the characteristic Mesopotamian fringe—which emphasize the close cultural connection between Scandinavia and the Middle East. To find, then, the Tollund Man wearing a cap of traditional "Phrygian" cut is not surprising.

In Anglo-Saxon, then, the new word *cæppe* must have meant a small, round hat—the meaning that the word bears today.

A brief word on this hat: made famous for us moderns when the first French Republic adopted it as the symbol of freedom. It provides us with a good example of how any ordinary, useful object—in this case an ordinary working-cap—may be endowed with a symbolic character. "The head-dress of the Persian Monarchs," Layard notes in his *Nineveh*, "appears to have resembled the Phrygian Bonnet or the French Cap of Liberty."

Greek, man's, c. 570 B.C.

The cap of this particular type became the symbol of liberty because, when a Roman or Latin manumitted his slave, he made the man a present of a cap, as a symbol of the ex-slave's newly acquired freedom. And though hats were not generally worn by men in the Roman state—Servius considered it a matter of reproach to the Phrygians that they "dressed like women," because they wore hats—a newly-manumitted slave used to wear, for some time after his being freed, the cap which proved his rank of freeman.

Of course, it was because hats and caps had fallen out of use among the Romans that a cap—any cap—could acquire a symbolical value. In the countries where caps were worn, this type of cap had no other than a practical purpose; and before the Greeks gave up wearing hats, the Phrygian cap was to be seen, along with a number of other basic types.

On Greek vases of the Archaic period, we may see all of these basic, and still worn types of hat:

The Parson's—small round crown and wide flat brim.
The 1916 British Steel Helmet or Fairycake—now worn by American Military Police.
The Robin Hood (with a stalk on the crown, such as is found on a Basque beret).

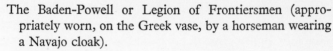

Greek, man's, c. 500 B.C.

The Baden-Powell or Legion of Frontiersmen (appropriately worn, on the Greek vase, by a horseman wearing a Navajo cloak).

The Girl Guide (though carried by men).

The Phrygian Bonnet—in its most exaggerated form, complete with "havelock" and long ear-pieces, obviously designed to tie under the chin.

Amazon wearing "Phrygian" bonnet, c. 480 B.C.

In this Greek vase-painting, which dates from *circa* 480 B.C., the Phrygian cap is worn by an Amazon woman, who is dressed in a tight-fitting, belted, trousered suit, the bodice of which is closed by what looks astonishingly like a zip-fastener.

The purely utilitarian form of peaked headwear that we English-speaking peoples have come to call the "cap" essentially consists in a crown with an added "peak" or visor; and, in its form with a flattened top, introduced about 1800, it is certainly now worn more widely than any other type of headgear—but no longer for utilitarian reasons.

Distinguished from the other "peaked" type of headwear, in which the front part of the brim has been flattened or projected to form a "visor," the peaked cap is basically a hemispherical cap to which a flat piece of stiffened material, lunette-shaped, has been added, to shield the eyes from the glare of the sun.

Roman bronze "jockey's cap," 1st cent.

We should, therefore, expect to find it first in conditions in which there is not only intense sunlight, but where the wearer needs to be protected from that sunlight—and this is, indeed, the case. The finest example from the ancient world is a Roman charioteer's cap which, though made of bronze, is identical in shape (as it was identical in purpose) with the modern jockey's velvet cap: "professional" headwear so sanctified by custom that it is worn as naturally by jockeys in "communist" Czechoslovakia as it is in "capitalist" America.

The rotatory movement of the chariots, bearing the Green or the White colours, would be enough to induce a sort of vertigo; and the blaze of sunlight reflected from the swept dazzling sand of the arena must have added to the dizziness caused by the repeated turns of the race. It was necessary to

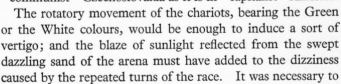

protect the charioteers' eyes from the sun's glare—and this
the practical Roman mind did by adding the flat peak to the
round charioteer's bronze or stiffened leather cap that the
Greeks of an earlier day were content to use.

Etruscan cap, man's, c. 500 B.C.

To some extent, this peaked helmet was adopted by the
Roman soldier; but not to any degree of generality. Useful
as the peaked helmet must have been, there were probably
reasons of social prejudice at work to prevent its wholesale
adoption.

In its original form, this peaked cap has come down to us;
not only as the aforementioned jockey's cap of modern use,
but the now standard British schoolboy's cap: the older form
of the "cricketing cap."

The other type of civilian cap, in which fullness has been
given to the crown, so that it can be flattened over the head, is
almost certainly of great antiquity, though it cannot be seen
represented in pictures earlier than those of Holbein; a number
of whose sitters, including the repulsive Sir Brian Tuke, wear
this peaked "golf cap."

Man's and boy's cap, c. 1890

But, in its third modern form—that is, with peak, headband and flattened top, the peaked cap has achieved a degree
of popularity rivalled only by the three-cornered hat of the
18th, and the top-hat of the 19th century.

This form was introduced at the beginning of the 19th
century, and can be seen illustrated in Sir David Wilkie's
well-known and once immensely popular painting of the
battle-field of Waterloo, where it is being worn by a surgeon
(a civilian, in those days before the establishment of a regular
Army Medical Service).

Here the flat-topped cap "just happens" to be worn on the
battle-field; this form of headwear was introduced as a civilian
mode, and for the first thirty years remained purely civilian.

Schoolboy's cap, c. 1820

It can be seen illustrated as a cap worn by sportsmen and
schoolboys: with the latter, indeed, it became *the* standard
headwear; both schoolboys and sportsmen having the cap
decorated with a long tassel-ended cord, springing from the
centre of the flat crown.

It became a cap for military use about 1830; being

introduced as an "undress" form of headwear. Indeed, the peaked cap did not become officially admitted to "full dress" until after the end of the First World War.

Still, once admitted to military use, the convenience of the peaked cap made it a sure stayer; and it had its influence on the choice of the shako as the standard headwear for British line-regiments, since the shako is only a peaked cap of more formal shape.

But, just because the military had adopted the civilian peaked cap, the civilian did not therefore abandon it. Civilians continued to wear it, even after it had been generally adopted by the Army, the Navy, the Merchant Marine, the Railway and the senior ranks of the Police. The crook who is being arrested by detectives in W. M. Frith's *Paddington Station* is wearing, with his Inverness and spats, a shiny-peaked cap of what now looks to us absurdly military cut.

Light Infantry, soldier, 1812

Civilians in Britain and America after about 1865 totally abandoned it—as had the schoolboys (from about 1850)—to the Army, Navy, Police and Railway, though it must be borne in mind that the peaked cap with the (relatively) soft, flat top, was reserved for the Army; Navy, Police and Railway wearing what was, in effect, a low-crowned shako.

The influence of private enterprise in establishing a standard uniform for the Merchant Marine must not be overlooked. Such lines as the Union and the Castle, being newcomers in the field, wished to give themselves "standing," and insisted that all their officers and cadets should wear a uniform as near to that of the Royal Navy as the law would permit. The sailors, too, were put into uniform, where, before, a merchant seaman wore what he liked—or, rather, what he could afford.

The officers of the Union and Castle lines—both of which had secured Royal Mail contracts—wore a cap with a japanned leather peak and a soft top smaller than is found today. There is no doubt that the example of these two shipping lines did much to standardize the costume of the merchant sailor all over the world, and did much to spread the cult of the peaked cap.

Greek helmet, c. 480 B.C.

But, if the peak was originally added to the round cap on

purely utilitarian grounds, the peak—by itself, as distinct from the cap to which it was added—became a symbol of command, at least in the Armed Services and in the Merchant Marine.

This is evident from the fact that, utilitarian or not, the peak—and not the gold-braid—was the one feature which distinguished the pill-box-with-peak of the officer from the pill-box-without-peak of the other ranks; for it should be added that, as the peaked cap, even though still "undress," began to become more and more "formal," so it tended to stiffen up. In certain regiments, the peak was edged with gold in the case of officers, and with brass in the case of other ranks.

An attempt has been made to distinguish among the peaked caps; for it is intolerable to a certain type of mind that it should be impossible to distinguish between the peaked cap worn by the General and that worn by the Commissionaire.

French képi, *modern type*

General MacArthur's huge and lavishly decorated cap has often been put forward as a striking example of this misguided attempt to emphasize the assumed importance of the wearer by over-emphasizing the dimensions of the cap; but MacArthur's efforts seem timid when compared with the efforts of those who have designed the caps for the Italian Army and riot-police, the Brazilian Air Force and the Shah-in-Shah of Persia. It is obvious that, whereas, when peaks were reserved to officers, the "magic" resided in the peak— so that there was a tendency (cf. the first Lord Beatty's highly individual naval cap) to exaggerate the normal dimensions of the peak—a tendency noticeable among Italian senior officers of the same date—the emphasis today, among rank-conscious peaked-cap-wearers, is to exaggerate the diameter and, often, the thickness, of the flat top.

The really gross exaggerations are still to be seen abroad, but it was in this country, round about 1924 (a year notable for a revival of the Ascot topper among young men) that the tendency to thicken the top of the cap was first noted.

Other ranks had been given the hitherto-reserved-for-officers peak with the Haldane Army Reforms of 1908: far-reaching reforms which included a complete redesigning of the British Army's "working" uniforms—the full-dress being left unaltered until the outbreak of war in 1914 put them into moth-balls for ever.

Since, apart from material—olive-drab twill or covert for the officers, khaki serge for the other ranks—there was nothing to distinguish the officer's cap from that of a man, work on making the distinction clear was undertaken immediately on the outbreak of war.

It is a fact of no little social significance that the alterations to "issue" caps were made not by the regulars, but by the temporary gentlemen, who set the military fashion-notes from 1914 to 1919, and who were responsible for, to quote but a few things, the "Charlie Chaplin" cane, "the Charlie Chaplin moustache," the wristwatch, the turn-up ("cuff," in America) on the uniform trouser-leg, and—which most interests us here—the individually-styled officer's cap.

In the contemporary idiom, this special war-time cap was known as a Gor Blimey, from its resemblance to the over-one-ear type of cap supposedly favoured by the Cockney coster-monger.

The Gor Blimey was made—or attained—by removing the grummet from the top of the cap, and then as much of the wadding as individual taste dictated. A sort of Apache cap was the result.

Though there was a ritual significance in this cap-mutilation —seen in an even more exaggerated form among the fighter-pilots of the Battle of Britain period—one could always put forward a "practical" reason for the mutilation. A soft-topped cap was not as liable to get blown off by the wind; it did not catch on the lintel of a dug-out's entrance; it could be folded and put in the pocket.

The Gor Blimey has passed out of use in the British Army, but it has been adopted—on the grounds of its supposed utilitarian advantages—by the American police, both metro-politan and rural.

By about 1922, the situation, cap-wise, was the same as in 1913: it was a situation in which only the material of which the cap was made effected the distinction between the cap of the officer and the cap of the other rank. The officers needed a distinctive dress; and the first move in that direction came when the Guards officers contrived to get themselves into khaki plus-fours.

That fashion did not last long, but fashion had also been busy at the officers' other ends: the top of the cap began to thicken and stiffen; the headband to grow deeper, the peak to grow longer, squarer and to lie more in a horizontal plane.

This is the type of military cap which has now been issued to all ranks for their walking-out dress, and has—since it has been sanctified by being just that much out-of-date—been adopted by the troops of the Russian Empire.

But one regrets the really distinctive cap adopted by the Russian troops during the "revolutionary" period. Consciously historic in inspiration—it was the cloth version of the helmet of Catherine II's guards—this cap was based on the helmet of the ancient Scythians, just as the badge of the "new" Russia—the Hammer and Sickle—is based upon something more ancient than the Czardom that Soviet Russia has replaced.

It was a pity that the Scythian military cap had to be replaced by the 1924 Sandhurst: the Scythian, old as it was, was the one original creation of nationalism to have come out of Europe since the French "volunteers" in the reign of Louis XIV returned from Croatia, with their handkerchiefs tied around their necks *à la cravate* (or "in the Croatian mode"), and gave the world the collar-and-tie.

Chapter Three

WOMEN'S HEAD-COVERINGS, ANGLO-SAXON TO THE MIDDLE AGES

A PART from hats worn ritually, women did not wear hats—as distinct from extensions of the head-covering —from the fall of Crete to the middle of the reign of Queen Elizabeth I. Say, from about 1200 B.C. to about A.D. 1570: a period of nearly two thousand years; and even then it is not certain that the hats that we see represented on Minoan statues and in frescoes at Knossos and elsewhere in Crete were not reserved to priestesses and their attendants.

*Minoan, woman's, c.
1500 B.C.*

But hats they were—as differentiated from mere head-coverings—as much as the object that the Babylonian Moon-Goddess wears on a seal is a hat.

These female Minoan hats are very interesting: as interesting as the dresses that the women wear. Flounced, with a far-thingale, in the Western mode of 1880, or bell-shaped, with a low neck and high-standing collar, in the mode of a dance-frock of the mid-1930s, the Minoan women look so "modern" to us that their art is of all ancient arts the most fascinating.

The woman who wears the bell-shaped dress, with the high collar emphasizes the "party dress" theme by wearing a conical, pointed hat, with a slightly forward tilt to the point. The hat is banded in horizontal stripes, and looks exactly like a hat from a Christmas cracker. The lady in the flounced skirt with the farthingale wears a hat with the brim turned up all around, though more so in the front than at the sides. This hat has a high, slender crown, and the underside of the brim is richly embroidered. In the case of the latter woman, there is no doubt that she is a priestess, for in each hand she is grasping a live snake; and a priestess, too, is another snake-handling lady, whose round, flat cap, with soft, red crown and blue-embroidered yellow turned-up brim, is exactly like that worn by the Knave of Hearts.

28

There is no positive evidence that hats were worn by women in Crete, save on ritual occasions. In the Early Babylonian period, *circa* 1900 to 1600 B.C., women most certainly wore both cap and hat, for everyday dress. In the case of the cap, this was a close-fitting affair, probably made of linen or some such thin material, with a cloth band or veil rolled around it. The hat was an elaborate conical tiara: very like the one that we have seen worn by the Minoan lady of approximately the same date.

But, from the end of Crete onwards, until Elizabeth's reign, women gave up hats.

Throughout East and West, the hat—and the cap, too—had been forbidden, by what seems a near-universal taboo, to women. If women wished to cover their heads, they either draped a part of their outer garment over their hair or wore some sort of separate hood or veil.

Assyrian, man's; c. 1000 B.C.

Our word "wife" meant originally "the veiled one"; and the basic meaning seems to hint at a custom similar to yashmak-wearing. That the veil was associated with not only femininity but marriage is not only proven by the fact that a woman's neck and ears were not bared in public until the turn of the 14th century but by the ritual insistence, as explained in the *Black Book of Arundel*, that a Queen of England must go veiled to her coronation.

Under the influence both of women and of the weather, men adopted the hood, as we shall see later. But here, dealing with the hat-fashions of Anglo-Saxon times, it must be emphasized that women wore only veils, secured, in the case of the humbler folk, by a fillet of "fancy worked" cloth or even plain cord; in the case of the high-born, by a fillet of gold or of gold-embroidered thread, the wonderful remains of which have been found in many a Saxon tomb; notably in the lead-coffins turned up recently by a bulldozer on the site of the Saxon royal town of Lyminge.

In the case of the rich, these veils were either of fine linen or of silk, and the jewelled fillet indicated social rank by its stones and/or metal. Silk was known to our Anglo-Saxon forefathers, even in the 7th century, for Pope Boniface, in

Roman woman at funeral, c. 450 B.C.

625, sent King Edwin "a shirt, with one gold ornament, and
one garment of Ancyra"—another hint of how Middle Eastern
goods were coming into England.   To Queen Ethelberga,
His Holiness sent a "silver looking-glass and a gilt ivory
comb."

But the numerous remains of silk found in the Anglo-
Saxon graves, even those of an early date, show that, for all
that silk had begun to be manufactured in the West only since
553, when two Nestorian monks had smuggled silk-worms
out of China in their hollow staffs, a Western silk-industry had
grown up on such a flourishing scale that the hand-block
printed silks from Southern Europe were a staple article of the
European "luxury" trade as early as the middle of the 7th
century.   One may imagine that, if too costly for dresses, the
Anglo-Saxon ladies found the printed silks ideal for the fillet-
bound head-dresses that custom ordained.

Now there are two forms of hat which appear in Anglo-
Saxon art after the "conversion" of Ethelbert and his Ten
Thousand Men of Kent.   One is a sort of coif—or "baby's
bonnet" without the chin-tie—which is seen on most of the
figures on the Franks Casket (a swordsman, killing another,
wears a Phrygian bonnet); the other is a round, tight-fitting
cap, worn "straight," and not on the back of the head, as a
skull-cap is worn.   In the clearest representation of this cup-
shaped cap—an Irish Christian bronze figure in the British
Museum—the cap is shown with deep ribs, the ribs radiating
from the centre of the cap; and it looks as though the cap were
either knitted or woven in rush or heavy cord.   Had this
Irish bronze been the only representation of such a round
cap, it would not have been possible to suggest that the Anglo-
Saxons wore such a head-dress; but fortunately, the same hat,
though not with such detail, is represented in sculpture in the
church of Bradford-on-Avon; the two angels flanking the
Crucifixion are both shown as wearing this hemispherical
cap, with what appears to be a head-band of some light material
tied twice round it, the ends of the veil hanging free behind.

Indeed, this sculpture proves that we need not accept the
bronze-capped figure as specifically Irish, since a bronze

Saxon woman, 10th cent.

Christ, also "Irish," and also in the British Museum, is a re-production of the central figure in the Bradford-on-Avon Crucifixion. It would probably be more accurate to suggest that both the "Irish" bronze and the English stone sculpture derived from a common (and almost certainly Eastern) model.

Round cap, with stalk, c. 1200

The Mediterranean sailor's cap—as worn by Edmond Dantès a long time later—appears in Byzantine art about this time. This is the well-known stocking-cap, with the edge rolled up to form a "brim," and the pointed top falling over the wearer's ear, the end of the cap being adorned with a tassel. The figure of David rescuing the lamb from the lion in the well-known Psalter, now in St John's College, Cambridge, *may* be wearing one of these pointed hats, but the drawing is so conventionalized that it is not possible to be more definite. However, the intimate connections with Golden Middlegarth—as the Northmen called Byzantium—were so close that it is unlikely that so handy a form of headwear as the stocking-cap should not have made its way to England.

Before we come to the Conquest, with another introduction of Continental ideas, and an even stronger reinforcement of Byzantine influence on art and fashions, we should take note of the fact that the crown, in a form closely approximating to its modern one, now makes its appearance in art.

The figure of Christ at Bradford-on-Avon is wearing what is obviously a crown, and not a hat and, as a curious indication of origin, his "kilt," with its regular flounces and farthin-gale-like girdle end, bears a suggestive resemblance to the dress of the Minoan Snake-Goddess, and a manuscript of Canute's time shows an angel crowning the King with a crown which is distinctly hooped.

It is clear that, under the influence of foreign ideas, the kings were abandoning their simple fillets or headbands of gold for the crenellated or floriated crowns as depicted in late Anglo-Saxon art.

To go a little beyond this period: there came a reaction against this elaboration of the crown. Not only is Harold shown in the Bayeux Tapestry as wearing a crown which is little more than a fillet, but the bronze figure of Christ attached to the cover of "A Lytle Booke with a Crucifixe," on which the Sovereigns of England took the Coronation Oath before the Reformation, is wearing a domed hat, bound round with a twisted head-band rather like a turban, and with a stalk on top of the hat.

But the relatively simple, "homely" culture of the Dano-English, which reached its apogee under King Canute, was doomed to make way for a Norse-Frankish culture more in keeping with the larger ideas of the age.

Europe, after the uncertainty of the Dark Ages, had found a chance of stability in the establishment of states based upon a conscious nationalism. Feudalism had come to support kings, and a strong Papacy had given the kings moral as well as legal sanction.

When Charlemagne had had himself crowned Emperor of the Romans at St John Lateran, on Christmas Day, 800, he had set a fashion in kingship.

The simplicity of the fillet was doomed. The new type of king wanted something grander than that; just as a grander form of crown he wanted a grander form of kingship. It is noteworthy that kingly splendour begins among the Teutonic nations as the old electoral idea departs from kingship.

And, just as Diocletian, in order to bolster up his own authority, tricked out his imperial dignity in Oriental, un-Roman diadems and purple robes, so did the kings of the new Church-stabilized Europe look East to find new ways of impressing the feudalized mob, and sustaining their own power by an excess of regal splendour.

Of all the gewgaws that Policy found to fix the bonds more firmly on the Ruled, nothing served its purpose better than a hat.

Call it a crown, call it tiara, call it diadem, call it what you will: though it be made of gold, and be covered with gems, it is still a hat.

Byzantine Imperial crown, c. A.D. 960

Nothing, in all the symbols that ambitious men have sought to endorse and magnify their authority, has equalled in potency the crown—the head-covering *par excellence*. Orb, sceptre, sword of justice or sword of mercy, ampulla, ermined robe, girdle, ring, sandals: none of these has ever been able to symbolize kingly authority as has the crown.

We have come to the end of the first great period of English history. With the coming of the Normans, everything will change.

William of Normandy and his men were a hatless crew: the Bayeux Tapestry shows them as wearing little hair (they shaved their heads at the back) and sporting caps which barely cover the top of the head—that is, when they are wearing hats.

William himself did not introduce an age of the Hat: it was William's coming which did that. It was not until after his death that men and women began, all of a sudden, and whole-heartedly, to cover up their heads. Only children went about with their heads free of enveloping hoods.

But for the relatively short reign of William the Conqueror, it was the Hat, and not the Hood, which covered the heads of Norman and English alike.

Between the fall of Knossos and the accession of Elizabeth I, women did not wear hats. This remark is a generalization, to which, of course, exceptions can be found—though not, it may be said, many.

One of these exceptions should be noted, for though it was designed to do service as a hood it was still a true hat, though a hat with ear-pieces.

It is flat, completely round, with straight sides which are a little wider apart at the top. Two triangular pieces of cloth are stitched at each side of the hat, within the "sweat band," and these two triangular pieces are wide enough at the top to cover ears and cheeks while tapering off sufficiently so that the ends may be tied under the chin.

Four hundred years later we shall encounter this arrange-ment, but with the hat perched separately on a head covered with a coif. Here, in this Norman ear-flapped hat, we have the coif as part of the hat; and if it may be argued that this is not a true hat (because it has ear-pieces) it cannot be argued that it is a hood, for all that.

3—H.H.

Norman knight, of 11th cent. A.D.

It is plainly a hat, and its shape raises a puzzling question: what inspired it? For, except for the materials of which it is made, and the embroidery which runs around the nearly vertical edge, the hat with its ear-pieces exactly resembles the flat-topped round helmet which was worn by Norman knights over a hood of mail.

The classic "Norman" helmet, seen on the Bayeux Tapestry —sugar-loaf top, with "nose-piece"—had given place to the flat-topped casque, worn over a hooded chain-mail "combination suit."

Which came first: the lady's pork-pie, or the knight's? It is not an unusual thing—especially in the past—for a male fashion to inspire a female one; but, on the other hand, the reverse has happened, even with tough Service personnel. One recalls that our commissioned naval officers—and, indeed, all the world's commissioned naval officers—wear a uniform originally deriving from a coat-and-skirt worn by a Duchess of Richmond.

On further consideration, however, it seems reasonable to suggest that the two forms, female hat and male helmet, both derived from a single model: the hat, of identical form, worn by both the Emperor and Empress of the East (as well as by some Byzantine court-officials) at the end of the 11th and the beginning of the 12th centuries.

Apart from this exception, the no-hats-for-women rule was unbroken; though a certain preoccupation with elaborate hair-dressing—braiding with ribands, entwining with flowers, as well as the use of considerable quantities of false hair— hints, during this restless period, at that sort of head-consciousness which usually leads to hat-wearing.

The veil continued to be the principal, and soon it was to be the only, head-covering for women; but with the coming of the Normans it acquired a new name as well as a new shape.

Byzantine Emperor, c. 1080

Called *couvre-chef* ("head-cover")—a word that the English anglicized to "kerchief"—the new type of "veil" was smaller than the Saxon "head-rail." Either rectangular or part of a circle, the *couvre-chef* was so arranged, that one edge hung over the forehead like a "bang" or "fringe," while the rest of the *couvre-chef* hung down at the back of the head, the ends often being crossed over the throat in front, thus virtually "enhooding" the face. One may understand how easy was the transition from the wearing of the *couvre-chef* to the wearing of a hood.

Woman, c. 1100

The hood itself came in just a little later than the mid-12th century, though, like all other fashions, it did not come in overnight, and universally. And, like all other fashions, it was anticipated, just as, when the fashion went generally, it hung on in odd places, and with odd people.

But it came in, if we must give it a year, about 1160; and in the century which had passed since the Conquest, some new hats had made their appearance.

The "Phrygian bonnet" had survived the Conquest—it was to continue to be worn right into the 13th century; as had, for eminently practical reasons, the hood attached to the cloak (something that, as the 11th century dawned, had become unfashionable for women).

But now hats of several shapes make their appearance: hats both large and small. We have a black felt hat, with wide, flat-brim, and low, flat-crown, sometimes shown in contemporary illustrations provided with tie-strings, sometimes not. It is surely only by accident that this hat, of so ancient a type, does not appear earlier, for it is one of the really "basic" hats of mankind. Here, in Norman times, it is the descendant of those broad-brimmed hats that men wore in Ancient Greece, and the ancestor, not only of the immense variety of 17th and 18th century hats, but also of the topper and the bowler of today.

Another hat—cap, rather—which appears often in contemporary drawings is a small, round cap with a stalk. We have seen it on the bronze figure on "A Lytle Booke with a Crucifixe," where it has a turban-like headband; but though some of the illustrations hint at decoration around the lower edge, none shows it with a headband. It is, though, sometimes shown, like the wide-brimmed hat, with tie-strings.

Wide-brimmed, c. 1200

The Hood, too, as an independent article of clothing, now makes its unequivocal appearance. We have seen how the separate hood is suggested on the Franks Casket; and it is probable that the separation of the hood from the mantle occurred earlier than the period which lies between 1060 and 1160. However, here it is, plainly attested; and as we encounter the coif with it, it is evident that a headwear fashion has come in which is to last until the end of the 17th century (and, in the conservative realm of the Law) until today. This is the fashion of covering the head—entirely—with some tight-fitting cloth wrapping, and wearing a hat, when the hat is worn, over this tight-fitting wrapper.

Coif, 13th cent.

The Coif has recently been re-introduced for adult wear, in the form of the waterproof hoods, with tie-strings, for protecting women's hair and/or hats from the rain. The Coif is, in effect, a "baby's bonnet," with strings, and after its introduction, at the latter half of the 12th century, it remained in ordinary use until about the middle of the 15th century, after which it was retained, as a professional form of headwear, by Medicine and the Law.

The Hood, which lasted longer than the Coif—in Germany, it lasted, in various forms, until the mid-16th century—was a pointed cowl with a cape whose ends reached the shoulders (as it appears to be shown on the Franks Casket). During the 12th century, the ends of the cape, which must for a long time have been pinned together for convenience, were permanently joined together, and the hood had then to be put on over the head, the joined-up shoulder-length cape now being known as the gorget.

Occasionally, the ends were left unjoined, in which case the two halves of the "gorget" were fastened with brooch or clasp.

We have here, though in cloth, the "Balaclava" of the mid-19th century onwards.

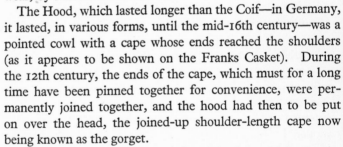

Gorgeted hood ("Bala-clava"), 1916

Before we go on to consider the other hats which appear in MSS and frescoes of this date, we could ask: what was the origin of the Hood (and Coif)? Many suggestions have been put forward: the principle—based, apparently, upon a remark of the Knight of La Tour Landry to his daughter, concerning the fleas which can jump off a neighbour's hair into her own—

that both Hood and Coif gave protection against vermin. I think that they gave protection against vermin, certainly, but a study of the development of both forms of headwear shows clearly that the development was as "natural" as that development in the frock-coat which led to the tail-coat. The loose, flapping ends of the cape were pinned together, until, one day, it occurred to someone—possibly a tailor, possibly not—to fasten them together permanently, and to slip the Hood over the head. The Coif, again, may be thought to have derived from a short-caped or capeless hood, which was provided with strings for extra security of fitting.

"Combed" bonnet,
English, 11th cent.

Whatever their origin, Hood and Coif were to have a long life, and to give rise to that curious fashion of the late Middle Ages for the "double standard" in hatting: the "outer" hat, for outdoors wear, and the "inner" hat which was never removed in public. In certain archaic forms, this double hatting has remained with us: one of the most common forms being, as we shall see later, the prelate's skull-cap worn under the mitre, and left in position when the mitre is removed.

Some other hats of this period have an extraordinary interest, in that they seem to be not merely type-anticipations of later models, but actual reproductions of them.

There is, for example, a version of the small round cap with stalk, already mentioned. This other version has a rolled brim, and may appear with or without the stalk. With or without its stalk, the hat bears a striking resemblance to the woollen hat worn in many modern sports, notably that of ski-ing.

Another 12th century hat with a startlingly modern look is a hat, of regular form, having a low, oval crown, surmounted by a knob. In an illustration of *circa* 1200, a pilgrim is depicted as wearing one of these hats over a closed hood; and in this version of the hat, it is shown as having a double brim, like that of the modern "double Terai," a hat that it resembles in general form as well as in the possession of a double brim.

"Double Terai,"
13th cent.

It appears to have been popular in the last quarter of the 12th century, and in its most regular form would not look out

"Beret," 13th cent.

of place on the head of a modern polo-player or big-game hunter.

From the "hard" appearance of this "solar topee," it is apparent that it was moulded over a hatter's block, in felt stiffened up with animal glue.

Yet another hat of astonishingly familiar form is the stalked soft cap, resembling a type of beret which has been popular with women over the past twenty years. It is rather fuller than the "traditional" beret, and does not fit—except at the headband—closely to the head.

The fillet, of gold and silver, often jewelled, continued to be worn by nobles, and there is evidence that the wreath, of precious metals, first encountered in Roman Imperial times, had been introduced (probably from Byzantium) for the festive occasions of Norman notables.

This period, too, marks the emergence of the flat bonnet, with (usually red) velvet crown, and turned up brim of fur, which, in varying proportions, was to remain in use, especially among the servants of royalty, for several centuries.

One may mention here that it has been suggested that the coif originated as a head-covering to be worn beneath chain-mail, and was thus, in the first place, an item of military clothing, adopted by the "civvy." It was probably adopted, if this attribution be correct, through the soldier's custom of keeping the coif in place when he threw off the hood of chain-mail.

The coif looked neat and workmanlike—and the "civvy" copied it.

The flat, "pill-box" hat, with ear-pieces, already mentioned, is often called, by writers on clothing, a "coif." This seems a permissible description, since the "hat" is never seen without its ear-pieces, save when worn by men; the ear-pieces, by the way, being known, collectively, as a "barbette."

If, inside of a barbette formed of two pieces of material attached permanently to the inside of the hat, a loose piece of cloth were looped around the chin, and the two ends attached to hat-brim or head-dress, this piece of cloth was known as a "wimple."

Woman's cap with barbette, 12th cent.

Women, too, wore a "gorget": it was a wimple which hung in front of the chin, rather than beneath it; and was often—though not always—tucked into the neck of the gown. It properly belongs to a later period than that under survey; and we shall have more to say of both wimple and gorget later.

Jew's hat, c. 1325

A hat-curiosity belongs to the beginning of the 13th century, to which we are now coming: Jews were ordered to wear a distinctive type of hat, with low, round crown and nearly flat brim, but with a knobbed stalk projecting upwards from the centre of the crown. To the Middle Ages, there was nothing so distinctive about a man as his headwear. *Le Chapeau—c'était l'Homme!*

Before, though, we leave the immediate post-Conquest period, we must notice a military helmet of unusual type. It appears to be a conical helmet, with a round knob at the point; the conical crown being set within a deep brim with vertical sides.

It is a helmet of unusual type, and, in this exact form, is not encountered either before or since.

Jew's hat, simpler form

About a century after the Conquest, we come upon the first evidences of a fashion which was not only to become a craze lasting over several centuries but to have a profound effect on the development of the Hat out of the Hood. This fashion—"Dagging"—was a crude form of vandyking, and is supposed to have originated in a conventionalized representation of the knight's battle-ribboned surcoat. That's as may be, but when "dagging" came in, about 1170, it was to remain popular until about 1500 (later in some parts of Europe), and, during the height of its greatest popularity, 1380–1440, it was to attain the proportions of a continental mania.

Soldier, c. 1100

Dagging first appears at the lower edge of the hood's gorget, and only some time later around the lower edges of body-garments. We shall see afterwards how this dagging of the gorget's edge was to produce some fantastic hat fashions in the mid-14th century.

I have seen it stated that, for a short period at the end of the 12th century, "women discarded their head coverings, and for the first time for generations they showed their hair."

Woman wearing fouriaux,
13th cent.

This remark is not quite accurate.   It is true that women did show their hair—very prominently, too—but they did not discard head-rail or *couvre-chef*.   Fashion, we know, is all powerful, but not when it is up against the opposition of a custom as powerful as that of veil-wearing.   The veil denoted rank, confirmed status: it is doubtful that women would have been permitted, by husbands or fathers, to discard the veil, even had they wished to do so.   They did not.

What they did do was to make their hair very noticeable, by parting it in the middle and dressing it in long plaits, or in tails enclosed in silk sheaths called *fouriaux*.   The *fouriaux* are usually shown, in contemporary paintings, as striped horizontally: red on a white ground.   The plaits were often lengthened by false hair or tow, braided with ribands and the ends decorated with jewelled ornaments.   Sometimes braids, as well as tails, were enclosed in *fouriaux*.   A loose veil, secured by a gold circlet, was worn with this style of hairdressing.   In the case of a queen, a crown was worn: it is said that Eleanor of Aquitaine it was who introduced this fashion of securing the veil with a crown.

What made this fashion extraordinary—and short-lived—was that it was only young girls who wore their hair uncovered, the tresses falling, braided or loose, from a centre parting.

It is true that adult women, in adopting this "young girls'" fashion, compromised with a light veil; but the essential foolishness of the fashion was its undoing.   By the end of the 12th century, women had adopted the wimple.

But, though the fashion of the two long plaits, hanging down over the breast, sometimes nearly to the shoes, lasted only about thirty years (1120–1150), the excessive hair did not vanish—that is to say, it was not cut off—and in getting it out of the way, women stumbled upon the origin of a whole new set of hair-fashions: hair-fashions which were to have their effect upon the development, first of head-dresses, and then of hats.

If one doesn't wish to cut hair off, there are many ways of disposing it neatly about the head   One may plait it, and twist the plaits around the head.   One may roll the plaits up

Head-dress: veil, fillet and gorgette, 14th cent.

into spiral "earphones," and pin them neatly at each side of the head. One may take the hair to the back of the head, and wind it into what the English call a "bun," and the French (less delicately but far more expressively) "en crotte de chevaux."

Coif and fillet, hair in crespine, 14th cent.

Now, had the modern hat-pin been invented—or, even, had the Roman matron's hair-skewer remained in use—the history of late mediaeval female head-fashions might have been very different.

But, lacking a proper means of securing the rolled-up hair, women had no alternative to putting the hair into little network bags, called *crespins* or *crespines*, the costliness of which varied with the wearers' purses.

Another fashion is noticeable at the time when the two long plaits are in evidence. Instead of securing the veil with a "head bend" (band) or even a complete circlet of gold, women would tie a band of linen over the veil, and around the head, letting the long ends of the band fly out as streamers.

During the first half of the 14th century, the crespine—the hair-retaining net (often ornamented with metal: but not, as often represented, of gold wire: gold wire not being known before 1380)—was what we may call a "fashion-pivot": the "basis" of a number of different head-arrangements. The crespine could be worn with barbette and fillet, or either barbette or fillet or both might be left off, many contemporary representations of fashionable women showing the hair covered with the highly ornamental crespine alone.

Hairdressing, by the way, was to provide its own aid towards establishing a fashion which was to persist until well into the 17th century: the hat widened to cover hair brought to the side of the face.

In the earlier part of the 14th century, women combed their hair from a central parting, plaited the two sides and coiled the plaits around the ears. Covered by crespin or veil, the coils of hair produced what were called, in contemporary phrasing, "bosses"—a term derived ultimately from military usage, through architecture.

Round cap with veil, man's, c. 1325

But round about the middle of the century, another

hairdressing fashion appeared: instead of coiling the plaits, the women doubled them, so as to produce vertical braids framing the face with two straight lines: a severe, regular appearance that the artists eagerly seized upon to portray, though in what must be considered a somewhat exaggerated style.

Fillet, barbette, hair in crespine, 14th cent.

To support these side braids, a fillet was worn, to which the braids were pinned, and though the hat for women was not yet reintroduced, the persistence of this hairdressing style affected hat designs when hats came in.

Many of the 14th century brasses still to be found in English churches show the arrangement of the braids and fillet; and often the face on the brass looks the more constricted for being enclosed, not only within its mathematically rigid vertical plaits but within precisely and symmetrically folded wimple and veil.

A mid-century description of a tournament, and (particularly) of the ladies who attended, seems to make it clear that the fashion of the "turban hood" or "turban chaperon" sprang from a usage common to both sexes.

The ladies are described as being "dressed in particoloured tunics, one-half being of one colour and the other half of another, with short hoods *and liripipes which are wrapped about their heads like cords. . . .*"

The "wrapped" liripipe, in the case of the men, was to become the true hat, succeeding the hood from which it derived.

The latter half of the 14th century is interesting to the student of the History of the Hat, for it is within this fifty years that women contrive to effect those changes in the traditional three-element headgear—wimple, fillet, veil—from which the true hat will emerge.

Woman wearing fillet, hair in templars, 15th cent.

As early as 1380, we have the so-called "cushion" headdress, which is a true hat in all but name and the consciousness of its being a modified veil-and-fillet. But the succeeding century will see the process accelerated, until, with the coming of the first Tudor, Woman has nearly recovered the hat that she lost in Crete and Phrygia.

The "goffering iron" is much in evidence in the latter half

of the 14th century. This was either a many-fingered curling-iron, which, when heated, imparted a wavy surface to a piece of starched linen, or consisted of two engaged cog-wheels, the spindles being hollow to receive the charcoal, which, when lit and puffed to red-heat, warmed the cog-wheels. The linen was placed between the cog-wheels, a handle was turned, and the "crimping" or "goffering" was done. One often hears of the "incredibly complicated" starched head-dresses of the past: with simple but effective machines to take the hard work out of goffering, there was nothing either complicated or incredible about the layers of goffered linen or gauze which made up the "complicated" head-dresses of the late 14th century.

Veil with gorgette, 14th cent.

A fashion belonging to the third quarter of the century was the so-called "nebula" (or, more properly, "nebuly") veil: in which goffering or "ruching" supplied a stiff framework for the face, and transformed the flowing veil, if not exactly into a hat, then certainly into a cap.

Sometimes, only the part of the veil above the forehead was ruched; sometimes, as we have seen, the whole face was framed in ruching; sometimes the ruched or goffered veil was worn over a fillet; and sometimes the complete edge of the (semi-circular) veil had its border stiffened with multiple parallel lines of goffering.

Again, the goffering over the forehead was so done that the "arch" was horizontal, with extensions to the fillet to support the forward edge of the nebula veil.

The fillet itself was "back." Not that it had ever gone out of use, but it had receded in fashion. Now it was prominently restored to favour, bringing with it a revival of an earlier fashion: that of the *fouriau*, the silken (usually striped) sheath for the plaits of hair. With this reintroduction of the fillet in a "stressed" form, it was seen at its most striking in the so-called "ornamental fillet," which had attached side-pieces resembling fretted or filagree pillars, which hugged the cheeks, thus giving a very rectangular shape to the face. Through these hollow side-pieces the hair was drawn: a trick which enabled the wearer to keep the side-pieces close to the face.

Where coronets were worn, they were made wide enough to fit over the side-pieces—and the exaggerated width given to the appearance of the face during this fashion's dominance is a striking characteristic of the period. The hair which was not contained within the side-pieces was carried to the back of the head, and there either confined in a crespine or hidden under a veil.

Padded roll, with veil, hair in caul, 15th cent.

Sometimes, instead of the fillet-with-side-pieces, an ornamental fillet or coronet was worn, to which braids of hair were attached, the braids forming "side pillars."

We have mentioned the "cushion," as coming very near to a true hat. This was the "padded roll," as worn by the men.

It was, in effect, the "brim" of the turban head-dress, with the cock's-comb and liripipe (in short, the entire "crown") removed.

This metonymical form of headgear—"the part for the whole"—is to be seen at all periods. The "padded roll" has returned once or twice within the past few years, and the crescent of feathers, serving for a "hat," had a long run among the less fashionable of our women, the fashion not even passing when the Russian lady discus-thrower was accused of stealing five of these feathery lunettes.

The important point to notice about women's hair styles in the latter half of the 14th century is that the hair was always kept rigidly disciplined. It was not so much that it was hidden, as that it was kept under tight control. Though a woman often drew her hair through side pillars, she used as often to show it, but the plaits which hugged her face were mathematically precise: as precise, indeed, as the side pillars which sometimes covered the tightly woven plaits.

It was not a "fluffy" age.

The "padded roll" was the harbinger of the hat-fashion's return, as far as women were concerned, but there was still something very hat-like about the fillets and side-pillars of metal or wire work. "A fret of golde she hadde next her heer," says Chaucer: and it was to be some time before the hair did not have a fret, crespine, caul, fillet or something similar, next to it.

There is one curious head-fashion observed in this period which deserves mention here, if only for the reason that it seems to belong to the same inspiration which gave the West its protracted turban fashion. This is the custom, among women, of shaving away the hair in front, so as to produce a high forehead. This fashion probably began by women's plucking away hair which "showed" beyond the edges of fillet and sidepillars. But, nevertheless, one is forcibly reminded, in reading of this custom, of the Mohammedan rule that the forehead must always be left bare, so that, in praying, a worshipper may touch the ground with his forehead. We may go even further, and connect up the realized "Orientalism" of the shaved-forehead custom with another of the same period: the bongrace (a custom which had an even longer run than that of shaving the forehead).

The early bongrace was a loop of cord or riband which hung from the fillet so as to cover the forehead. It seems to have arisen because the fillet had become confused with the chaplet—and, in the 14th century and earlier, the chaplet or circlet designated the wearer as unmarried, while the wearing of a cap marked the matron.

The bongrace, like so many other articles of late mediaeval clothing, was used as the vehicle of certain sumptuary symbolism. For instance, if the bongrace were of velvet, it signified that its wearer was in enjoyment of an income of £10 a year and over.

Snobbish writers of James I's and Charles I's day, noting the unfashionable tastes of City merchants' wives, allude to the preference for the bongrace; so that this fashion lingered on well into the 17th century.

Chapter Four

THE HOOD

Hood with beginnings of liripipe, c. 1200

To speak of any fashion as "universally adopted" is to speak in hyperbole. One could not say, even of the 18th century, that "every man wore a three-cornered hat," or, of the succeeding century, that "every man wore a tall hat." It would be truer to say that every man wore a three-cornered hat in the 18th century than that every man wore a tall hat in the 19th century; but the first statement would still be untrue; and it would be just as inaccurate to say that, from about the middle of the 12th century, "every man wore a hood."

Contemporary drawings, paintings, sculpture make it clear that there were plenty of independent spirits who wore hats, and some of these are of extraordinary interest. All through the hood-wearing period, there are the many unhooded. One gets parties of men, in which as many go unhooded as hooded. And it is not at all easy to determine the rule—if rule there be —which lies behind the wearing and the non-wearing of a hood.

A suggestion is that the hood was originally an article from the wardrobe of the peasant, adopted by the upper classes for doubtless practical reasons. Few private houses had windows, and the division of the house into rooms had not been adopted: the mediaeval world must have been a draughty one, at the best of times.

Later, the upper classes were to adopt other things from the peasants' way of life: in particular, their dances. But starting off with the hood was enough to go on with: it was warm, it was or could be elegant, and it lent itself to the caprices of improvisation and experiment. On the other hand, there must have been some who so objected to the peasant origin of the hood as to refuse to wear it.

It may be. Look at a photograph of a group of men in the days when "every well-dressed man wore gloves—or a tie-pin

46

—or spats—or a silk hat." All the men may seem not only to be well dressed but of the sort which knows "what's done."

Half of them won't be wearing some "essential" article of clothing or personal decoration. It's the same with hoods: "everyone" wore them—but so many didn't.

Round cap, man's, c. 1200

So far as hats—and even hoods—went, the 13th century was not an innovating one. Not even a developing one, save in very timid ways. One of these ways was to bring women's hair to cover the ears, rather than to bun it at the back. When the fillet, a starched (and often goffered) linen circlet—like the modern parson's collar—began to be worn, the siting of the crespin-netted hair at the temples stretched the fillet to each side, and gave that "wide" appearance to the head which was to stay fashionable, on and off, until the reign of Mary Tudor.

As far as men's hats were concerned, the 13th century kept to what had been introduced or retained in the previous century.

The hood was "in," as was the "beret"—the round, soft hat with a stalk. The broad-brimmed travelling hat, with strings for hanging it over the back, was retained—it was too useful to have been let go. The "solar topee" and the "polo helmet" are in evidence in the illustrations of the time, but there is something new in the appearance of a hat like a small bowler.

What does depart. in this century, is the flat, round "pill-box" hat for men, though the shape is retained in women's head-dresses. Contemporary art also gives evidence of a "Japanese" hat, on the heads of peasants. That is to say, a hat—it seems to be woven or plaited (probably of straw)—in which there is no sharp angle between brim and crown, the brim and crown being "all of one piece." This hat is almost invariably shown as being worn over a coif—and here we must point out what seems to be a fact: that it was the lower class of men which tended to cover up the head with coif or hood. The fact that women did, also, and that, with women, there was a symbolic reason, rather suggests that the peasant was forced to adopt a female-type head-covering, if not by any explicit law, then at least by an inescapable social obligation.

Straw hat, worn over coif, 13th cent.

We must not forget that, already, the deep currents of change which were to abolish the feudal system were rising towards the placid surface of the Whitehall-patterned England of the 13th century: and no society is so much in evidence (as regards its outward forms) as when it is on the verge of inevitable disappearance. One feels that the workers were ordered by their lords to wear the hood as a mark of serfdom—which is why women also wore hoods (or their more complicated equivalents)—and why gentlemen tended to avoid them.

Yet, just as the speech and the dances of the vulgar eventually reach upwards and capture the "refined," so did the hood come to provide head-dresses for nobles and kings. But that was not to happen for more than a hundred years after the 13th century had ended.

Later, in this History of the Hat, we shall have cause to observe the widespread and long-lasting domination of the Wig: not as disguise for baldness, but as a head-covering in its own fashionable right. False hair has always been worn, as a sop to vanity, and wigs had been worn ritually by the priest-kings of many a nation of the Ancient East. The period, 1675 to 1800, was to see wigs worn by all classes of men.

We have already noted how the long plaits of the 12th century were often extended by false hair or tow. We now, in the 13th century, come across a women's fashion which, much more than the wearing of false hair, anticipates the 17th–18th century fashion of the wig, in so much as the wig is to be considered a form of headwear. This is the fashion of pinning the wimple to each of the crespin-confined cushions of hair at the temples, thus making the hair do duty for the fillet-with-barbette to which ordinarily the wimple would have been pinned.

There was a fashion, as the 13th century drew to a close, of wearing saffron-dyed wimples. The Cunningtons note this fashion, and quote a couplet from *Handlyng Synne*:

> *Wymples, kerchyves, saffrund betyde*
> *Yellugh under yellugh they hyde*

—but suggest no reason for the fashion. It is plain that the adoption of yellow for the wimple was, by contrast, to make the face appear whiter; though, the author of *Handlyng Synne* (who was a fault-finding parson) suggests that the faces looked still as yellow as ever. Of course, there may be another explanation of the fashion: a yellow face suggests jaundice, and jaundice was treated, in those days (and for long afterwards) by infusions of saffron.

It may be that the wimple was dyed with saffron as a sort of prophylactic against a recurrence of the jaundice. It can be noticed how often, in human history, the hat has been used to proclaim the wearer's allegiances, profession, hopes. Why not his—or, in this case, her—fears?

There were, however, some social significances in colour which have not been recorded. Certain colours are fashionable for limited periods, and equally they are unfashionable. White may well have been "out" with fashionable women at the end of the 13th century, just as brown (for hats) was "out" with fashionable men between 1900 and 1925—and, indeed, as far as the "hard felt" is concerned, has not yet returned to favour.

That colour was establishing itself as an inseparable element of certain ritual headwear is evident from Minot's remark, *circa* 1352, about "cardinalis with hattes rede."

The Byzantine influence was still strong, as far as women's headwear was concerned. Three centuries had passed since the sisters of the Emperor Basil II had married, the one, Vladimir, Grand Duke of Kiev, the other Otto II, Emperor of the West: yet, had this Byzantine penetration into Europe not been enough to sustain and to promote Levantine ideals and fashions, the close contact between East and West maintained by the Crusades would have kept Europe constantly conscious of the Near East. The fact that fashion was consciously affected by the admiration in which all classes held the East is forcibly demonstrated by the fact that an abrupt change of fashion coincides with the suppression of the Templars at the very beginning of the 14th century. The "pill-box" helmets, worn over a hood of chain-mail, to be seen on the recumbent effigies of the Knights Templars in Temple Church, London,

Byzantine court lady, A.D. 550

4—H.H.

Velvet and fur cap, over coif, 1325

and elsewhere, were worn, in softer materials, by women right up to the suppression of the Order, after which women are no longer seen sporting "Templar" hats.

But to return to the hood, for three full centuries the wear, if not of the fashionable, then certainly of the most numerous.

We find, even about the year 1200, that the hood, whether attached to the cloak or merely provided with a gorget (or "neck" to cover the shoulders) has already a well-defined backward-falling point. As the 13th century progressed, this point or "liripipe" tended to become more and more elongated, though it never became other than narrow. At its most exaggerated, the liripipe might be as long as four feet, and one cannot understand how it can ever have been other than a confounded nuisance—and often a danger (as when an enemy, coming up behind, could pull it, and render the wearer helpless). It is recorded that money was often kept in the liripipe —which must have rendered this extraordinary fashion an even greater danger to the wearer.*

In the drawing of the funeral procession of Sir Philip Sidney, in 1585, you may observe that the beadle wears a hood with a broad liripipe reaching down to his heels: and if the court-jester's cap and bells can be fairly accepted as the dress of the 14th century, then it lasted until the 19th century, when the Fulfords of Fulford were still employing their Fool —the last family to do so.

The liripipe was always made in one piece with the hood, and contemporary drawings show that with men at work, it was twisted around the head and the end tucked in, so as to form a sort of turban binding the crown of the hood. When, eventually, men came to discard the hood, they kept the turban into which the liripipe had developed—but that belongs to a later part of this history.

As I have said, the hood was like a "Balaclava," in that it was slipped over the head, the gorget fitting snugly over the shoulders. Women, too, wore the liripipe with their hoods, but, unlike those of the men, the hoods of women were always

* Another use is suggested by the obsolescent phrase "(to give someone) a good larruping."

provided with a vertical opening at the neck, which might or might not be buttoned up. Sometimes, in the absence of buttons, the two halves of the gorget would be wrapped over. Later, there is evidence that men's hoods had buttoned gorgets, but at this period the gorget's on men's hoods were closed.

There is another type of hood belonging to this period, the consideration of which garment must force our attention upon certain types of ecclesiastical headwear which found their ultimate forms hereabouts in time.

This other type of hood was the Amess (variant spellings, ammis, aumuses) which had the paradoxical quality that, though worn by both sexes of all classes, it was, in the popular estimation, somehow specifically associated with high degree: especially of the Church. "Ammys for a Channon," explains Palsgrave, translating the French word, *aumusse*.

The amess, Planché says, was "a canonical vestment, lined with fur, that served to cover the head and shoulders," and he points out that it was "perfectly distinct from the amice," called by Pugin, "the chief ecclesiastical vestment"—and itself originating in a head-covering.

But it was also "a cowl or capuchon worn by the laity of both sexes," and it seems probable that it was not its shape, but its combination of costliness and convenience which restricted it, firstly to the upper classes and secondly to the upper clergy.

It was worn by kings—*Pour 24 dos de Gris a fourrer aumuces pour le Roy*—and by ladies of the Court—*Pour fourrer une bracerole et une aumuse pour la dite Madame Ysabel* (both quotations from 1351), and, as Planché observes, "though peculiarly a canonical vestment, it was worn by all classes and sexes."

A reference to its use by monks has this to say: *ut almutiis de panno nigro vel pelibus caputiorum loco uterentur*, which truly barbarous Latin conveyed to the Middle Ages thus: "they shall wear on their heads amesses of black cloth or fur."

But, correctly, the mediaeval scribe should have written, "of black cloth *and* fur," for the amess was a fur-lined hood; and though it was usually made of black cloth, there is plenty of evidence that it was sometimes made in cloth of a less mournful hue.

The amess "formed a portion of the Royal, Imperial and Pontifical habit," and though the fur lining was usually grey, amesses for use in a cathedral chapter were lined with white ermine, and where the bishop was a temporal as well as a spiritual lord, his amess was not only with "spotted" ermine but had ermine tails sewn around the edge of the hood.

Contemporary drawings show the amess as a hood, fitting snugly about head and face, and with the gorget cut loose, to fall to about mid-breast. There is an indication that the crown of the amess was slightly "bi-cornute," or having two shallow protuberances rising vertically at each side of the face, but this probably only indicates that the soft fur-lined cloth has some form of two-horned headwear underneath.

The amess, like the linen coif (which was still being worn under heavy wigs by English judges up to the end of the 19th century) had a long life, but in its later period, it seems to have become grey both inside and out—that is to say, both cloth and fur lining were grey.

This seems evident from Skelton's reference:

> *Those words his grace did say*
> *Of an ammus grey*

—and Milton's:

> *. . . morning fair*
> *Came forth with pilgrim steps in amice grey.*

The 14th century saw some profound changes in hat-styles for men, while the head-dresses of the women also underwent some modification, though not as great as in the case of men.

The hood, with constantly lengthening liripipe, was still worn by the upper classes—it was to remain the "uniform" of the peasant until the economic results of the Black Death freed him from serfdom, and put an end to feudalism in England until after the World War of 1914–1918.

The coif was worn, especially by ecclesiastics, lawyers and soldiers, who had adopted it from necessity (as had the priests), but continued to wear it from habit.

The old shapes continued—the Sailor, the Bowler, the Robin Hood, the Beret, the Ice Hockey Player—but in new

"Polo" helmet, English, 12th cent.

and less simple guises. The feather, which, according to Hollywood historians, has ornamented every hat not definitely a hood from Attila the Hun's to Sydney Carton's, appears for the first time as a hat-decoration. By the end of the next century, this feather-fashion was to take on the proportions of a craze, with high prices being paid for the plumage of rare Oriental and African birds.

"Napoleonic" hunting hat, 1325

But, as early as the first quarter of the 14th century, it is clear that this feather-fashion is well "in"; and there is one miniature, dating from about 1325, which shows a knight going a-hawking who wears a hat entirely covered with the booty taken from a peacock-in-his-pride.

The interesting point about this miniature resides in the shape of the knight's sporting hat, which is evidently made of felt, on to which the peacock's feathers have been stitched. It is exactly the same shape as that of the campaign hats worn by staff officers on both sides during the Napoleonic Wars, and was evidently produced in the same way, i.e., by turning front and back of the brim upwards, joining them, and then cutting away the brim at the sides to achieve a roughly triangular outline. You may see the same hat today—though modestly decorated with gold braid, and not lavishly with peacock's feathers—on the beadles at the Bank of England.

The sugar-loaf, brimmed hat, with the brim pulled down in front to form a peak is a shape especially characteristic of the 14th century, notably of its first half. But the wide-brimmed hat, with an obtuse angle where brim joined crown, was still in favour, and was soon to be adopted, in steel, for men-at-arms.

But the greatest change came about through a new—a "lazy man's"—way of wearing the hood. (Or it may just have been the hot man's way.)

Instead of putting the hood over the head, and pulling the gorget over the shoulders, the *face-piece* was pulled over the head, leaving the liripipe hanging over one ear, and the (usually dagged) gorget over the other.

Now, it was obviously most inconvenient to have liripipe and gorget falling forward every time that one bent one's head: the gorget, then, was pulled up on to the crown of the

Merchant's, c. 1325

head, and the long liripipe whipped around it turban-fashion, the end of the liripipe being tucked away to secure the "turban."

The effect of whipping the liripipe around the gorget was to cause the dagged edge of the gorget to stand up like a cock's comb (and "coxcomb," as a term for an extravagantly affected dandy has its origin in the upstanding, dagged gorget).

Cunnington, in referring to this fashion, has a note: "1380–1420. Very common 1390–1410," but, in fact, this "turbaned-hood" is encountered in the first half of the 14th century, along with a "barber's-pole-striped" conical hat that we shall encounter again during the 18th century.

Planché, in his great *Cyclopaedia of Costume*, calls attention to the fact that the wearing of feathers in the hat was a fashion which is not encountered before the middle of the 14th century; but there was also another fashion which took its rise at about that time: the fashion of the decorated hat-band —itself to become eventually as important as, if not perhaps more important than, the hat that it adorned.   References to hat-bands are frequent from the middle of the 14th century until the closing years of the 19th century; and a whole etiquette and terminology arose, as we shall see, from the custom of wearing a piece of riband around the base of the hat's crown.

The first references to this fashion show that the extravagance to be seen in Tudor, Jacobean and Caroline hat-bands had not yet been envisaged: *Pro hatbandys de serico negro* [*sic*], *ijs* (1412–1413) is a far cry from *A hat-bande with xviij gowlde buttons* (1594), but the imaginative talent of the 14th century was concentrated on the possibilities of feathers and the "turbanizing" of the hood.   The hat-band could wait. . . .

Now, having stuck the crown of the head through the face-piece of the hood, and whipped liripipe around gorget to make a "cock's-comb," it was plainly more convenient not to have to repeat the adjustment of gorget and liripipe every time that one took off one's hood—and one had to do that pretty frequently: as frequently then as today.   More so, perhaps,

Round thrum cap, worn over hood, c. 1450

since men do not customarily raise their hats to other men in present-day England. *When thou comest by-fore a lorde . . . hod or cappe that thou of do:* there is a ring of something more than mere advice in the peremptoriness of this counsel.

Liripipe and gorget, than, were stitched into place; and the next step was just as inevitable: to save the maker the trouble of constructing a hood of one piece, and stitching it up into a "turbaned hood," the liripipe—now a padded roll—was sewn around the edge of a round cap, and within the padded roll a cock's-comb was stitched.

Small-brimmed hat, over hood, late 14th cent.

Two further developments were now possible: the "loosening" of the crown, to make what is known as the "bag crown" —a liripipe sort of idea, where the end of the crown fell over the edge of the padded brim. The other development was to wear merely the brim—or padded roll—without either crown or cock's-comb.

The padded roll did not need a crown: worn over a coif it would provide a brim for the coif, while the coif provided a crown for the brim. There is evidence, however, that the padded roll, or roundlet, was worn without any other head-covering, and thus came very near to being a sort of male counterpart of the girl's chaplet which, in the 14th century, designated the wearer as unmarried; the wearing of a cap marking the wearer as a matron.

These hats developed from the hood put on in a novel fashion had many contemporary names, of which "chaperon turban" and "twisted cock's-comb turban" are perhaps the best known. The fashion seems to have originated in Italy (It. *cappuccio*) which does not sound improbable, as the fashion obviously originated in a land where the heat would have rendered an overall head-covering unpleasant.

There are two curious hat-fashions belonging to this century which deserve mention here: one—belonging to the latter half of the 14th century—is the two-hat fashion, favoured by the elegant young men. A tall felt hat, with a band of fur around the lower edge, was worn on the head, while a wide-brimmed hat was slung over the back: "his hat heng at his back by a las," as Chaucer says.

The other curious hat-fashion was that of carrying it, rather

Round fur hat, late 15th cent.

than wearing it. This fashion comes again and again—we have had the hat-carrying fashion several times in our own day; the 18th and 19th centuries had their periods when hats were merely "chapeaux bras": hats designed to be carried, and never worn. But the 14th century "knuts"—curious that we have never replaced that outmoded phrase!—carried their hats aloft on their walking-canes.

There was a fashion, too, for sewing bells on hats—as on the points of the "pyked" shoes. The Fine Lady on the White Horse had, you will recall, "rings on her fingers and bells on her toes." The cap-and-bells of the jester dates from this passing fashion.

One hat-fashion which, in a vestigial form, has persisted to this day was that adopted by older professional men of passing the liripipe, its end decorated with "streamers" over one shoulder. As time went on, the liripipe grew smaller, until the "streamers" or bunch of ribands became a badge, still to be seen on the left shoulder of the French magistrate and on the robe of the Knight of the Garter.

The cockade, too, worn in the hats of liveried servants is, R. Turner Wilcox suggests, the vestigial relic of the roundlet with pleated and dagged-edged chaperon.

As early as the 12th century, it had been remarked that the English were copying the modes of Paris—not only in shape but in extravagance, but, by the end of the 14th century, the Burgundian influence in fashion, both for men and women, became very marked. The simple explanation for this is probably the true one: that we were fighting *with* the Burgundians, *against* the French. On the other hand, the famous French fashion doll, known to have been sent regularly from Paris to Venice as early as the 14th century, continued to arrive in England through the wars of the 18th century: political enmity between England and France not being considered a reason why the English ladies should forswear allegiance to French fashion.

High Burgundian cap, 1460

Whatever the reason, Burgundian influence in fashion is marked during the latter half of the 14th century (and it was probably through Burgundian intermediacy that the Italian

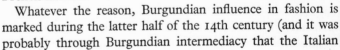

cappuccio came to England). The Burgundian contribution
to male and female fashion was in the shape of the tall hat:
Flaundrish bever hats, Chaucer calls them, though "beaver"
was often called "hair."

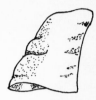

*High Burgundian
cap, 1460*

They were frequently dyed green, though it is not clear
whether such hats were what we now call "beaver"—i.e.,
beaver skin, with the fur outward—or of felt prepared from
beaver hair.

I think that they were of beaver felt, and not fur hats.

Italy, too, was doing a thriving export trade to Britain.
Trade relations between the commercial republics of Italy
and London and the great ports of Britain began early, and
had always been closely maintained, and the tall "steeple or
sugar-loaf" hat from the Duchy of Milan and other places in
Italy was very popular, though at a date rather later than that
which saw the Burgundian "mitre" fashionable. Made of
fine felt, wool cloth or "panama" straw, these tall hats were
known as "Milayne bonnets," and those who dealt in them
were known as "milayners"—our modern word, "milliners."

The word, bonnet, as applied to a man's hat, was not
definitely obsolete until the end of the last century—"I was
told to take off my bonnet, and tie a billy-cock tight down"
(*Life Among the Colliers, 1862*)—and to this day, a Scotsman
calls his head-dress a "bonnet." The word itself came from
ME *bonet*, a coarse green cloth from which "bonnets" were
made; and there seems to be a connection between this word
and the modern word for a coarse green cloth, *baize*.

Centuries of the Crusades failed to halt the progress of the
vast Saracenic army and finally the non-Byzantine West con-
ceded victory to the Turks.

Even as early as 1328, the "Turkish" fashion is to be seen,
especially among those who were in more or less of proximity
to the advancing Turk, or who dwelt in the cities in close
commercial relationship with the Eastern Mediterranean.
The splendid condottiere of Simone Martini has a "bagged"
bonnet, with a turned-up ermined edge, which is of decidedly
Oriental flavour; and as the 14th century progresses, hats, both
of men and of women, betray this intense preoccupation with

*Cap with rolled
brim, 1457*

the East—for all that the whole of Western Europe, especially
England, France and Burgundy, was involved in war.   Noticeable is the fact that this mental *Drang nach Osten* brings back
the old Byzantine court fashions as well as introduces the
"turban."   The fur hat that the City Swordbearer wears,
and which appears as the "crown" over the City of London's
coat-of-arms, dates from this time; is, in fact, the "mortar
toque" of the early 12th century restored—and that fashion,
as we have seen, probably owed itself to the Crusaders' contact with the Byzantine East.

Fur cap, man's,
c. 1430

Contemporary references to the Black Death make it clear
that, though its cause was unknown, its origin was felt to be in
the East, for it was in the ports handling the Eastern trade
that the plague first appeared.

Here again was something fearful to keep the East constantly
in men's minds—and, in symbolism of fashion, on their
heads.

The "turban" and the "padded roll" (itself the main part
of the "turban," shorn of its cock's-comb) harked Eastward;
but the fantastic fashion-changes that women were to know
as the century wore on were not less Oriental in extravagance,
as well as in inspiration.

The same thing was happening to the hood of the women:
though women were to retain the hood longer, they were on
the way, as men were, to a hatted condition.

Of course, religious ordinance, which had become even
more powerful by becoming social ordinance, was responsible
for the long retention of the veil.

Turban hat, with
"cock's-comb,"
early 15th cent.

As early as the beginning of the 3rd century, the ecclesiastical
authorities had—interpreting St Paul—ordered women to
cover their heads while in church, and this gave Christian
"sanction" to the veil, which was the mark of women's
servitude—"Wives, obey your husbands in all things . . ."—
throughout the Mediterranean, and all the lands tributary to
it.   The persistence of custom, having a moral force far
greater than any statute law, is shown by the fact that it was
only towards the end of the last World War that the then Pope,
Eugenio Pacelli, gave women who entered Roman churches

dispensation from the necessity of wearing hats or any other head-covering.

It is curious, reading the denunciation of extravagance in Chaucer's *The Parson's Tale*, to realize that this was not only an age of what, among us, would be called "total war," but an age of political and social ferment.

But the Parson gives such detailed description of the extravagance that it cannot all be a poor cleric's bile. Besides, the pictures of the time make it clear that dress had reached one of its most fanciful periods. "May not a man see as in our days," the Parson asks, "the sinful costly array of clothing, and namely in too much superfluity. . . ."

The parti-coloured hose, with "piked" toes eighteen inches in length, the long and short cote-hardies, houppelandes, garnaches and cloaks were not the only garments in which the taste for extravagance of cut and material showed. The hats, too, were no less fanciful than the garments below.

Chapter Five

DEVELOPMENT OF THE ECCLESIASTICAL
HEAD-DRESS

URING the first four centuries of Christianity, or, specifically until Constantine handed over the State religion with its temples, dioceses and ecclesiastical organization to the Christians, the Christian clergy wore the same clothes as the laity. Certain changes were made generally in the colours associated with religious, or solemn, occasions: whereas the "pagan" Roman maid wore a scarlet net or snood on the night before her wedding, a wreath of vervain and a saffron veil during the ceremony, the Christian girl forwent the scarlet net as being too reminiscent of the ritual scarlet net of the Vestal Virgins, and wore a purple or white veil. The purple veil has gone, but the white veil is worn today, not only by Christian women but by Jews, and, indeed, by women of no religion at all.

It is possible that the prim, not to say priggish, Christians abandoned the saffron-dyed veil because of the fact that the bright yellow wig was the trademark of the whore in Imperial times: when Valeria Messalina, wife of that Claudius who conquered Britain, slipped off to the brothel, she always wore a yellow wig.

But the clergy had no distinguishing mark of their calling until after their religion had been "established."

*Etruscan cap,
woman's,
c. 520 B.C.*

The Roman flamen, as we have seen, wore the Etruscan cap—the everyday headwear of those who had not only conquered Latium but had given the Latin tribal village its name, Rome, and its inhabitants their culture.

The head-dress of the flamen was also worn by his wife, and it consisted of woollen braid wound turban-wise until a tall, conical ("sugar-loaf") shape had been attained.

This "turban" was held in place by a twisted border or headband, and, of course, the Christian clergy wore nothing resembling it—so long as a "pagan" priesthood existed. It must be borne in mind that Constantine did not "abolish," the "pagan" priesthood—he merely "disestablished" it, leaving it theoretically free to continue to minister to the adherents of the Old Religion.

In practice, however, it was free only to submit to its aggressive rival or to face the consequences of "heresy." But not for some hundreds of years did Christianity, in Italy at least, feel able to embark upon an active extermination of the remains of "paganism"; and the Old Religion, for all that it had been deprived of its temples and landed property, was still functioning in the 7th century, after which time it vanishes as a "respectable" faith, and carries on in the mountain villages of Europe.

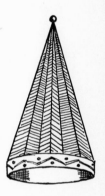

Papal tiara,
A.D. 540–604

It is, indeed, coincidental with the Old Religion's vanishing that, apparently for the first time, the Christian priesthood is seen wearing ritual head-dress—and, as we might have expected, it is the Etruscan "sugar-loaf" of the flamen, with only this slight difference: that the braids do not wind spirally upwards from "brim" to apex, but run vertically upwards. It is clear, from the careful drawing of this "mitre," which dates from the end of the 6th century, that it is based on the Etruscan mitre of the flamen, and that the variation is deliberate: and made so as not to under-emphasize the connection between Christianity and that "paganism" whose wealth, both temporal and spiritual, Christianity had inherited.

But, if this be the first appearance of an ecclesiastical hat in Christian usage, it is not the first example of priestly headwear: that is to say, headwear specifically devised to proclaim its wearer invested with priestly dignity and power.

The Christian priest's clothing may not have differed in form from that of the members of his congregation, but, unlike them he wore a fillet of white wool or linen, which encircled his head just above the ears, and from this fillet hung two bands of the same colour and material ("lappets"). This fillet, with its lappets, was the priest's badge of office: the outward and visible sign of his inward grace. These lappets still form a prominent (and to ritualists, a vital)

part of the Pope's tiara, and of the mitres of his sub-
ordinates.

Later, we shall see how the elaboration of this fillet-
and-lappets turned the simple band into a veritable hat,
and how this hat evolved into the bishop's mitre as we know
it.

But here a word on the effect of this absence of specific
priestly vestments on the development of Christian ecclesiastical fashion.

*Christian priest's
head-dress.   4th
cent.*

Wearing the same garments as their flock, the priests
inevitably kept up with the changes of secular fashion, and
a lamentable tendency was evinced on the part of certain
worldly priests to get a little ahead of "the latest." Several
Councils of the Church were provoked into condemning the
priesthood's "fashion consciousness," and the result of the
virtual banning of "fashion" was to halt, so far as priestly
dress was concerned, normal developments, so that ecclesiastical dress became "fossilized" in form. Just as there is
nothing intrinsically "legal" about the horsehair wigs of the
British and Indian justiciary—they are a civilian fashion of
the 18th century—so there is nothing but tradition to make the
vestments of a Roman priest "ecclesiastical": they are merely
the civilian dress of the 5th century.

In headwear, however, it was a different matter. Ritual
headwear was needed, in order to confer dignity on the holder
of the sacred offices—and as, apart from the broad-brimmed
petasus for travelling, the Italians of the first centuries A.D. did
not wear hats, hats had obviously to be developed or imported
from another land or another faith.

We have seen that the importation was done from the dis-
credited but still venerable Old Religion—a religion of rustic
animism, admirably suited to the farming community on
which the great Roman Empire had been erected.

Now, as to development, the fillet-with-lappets was to do
its share. First of all, it was worn over a white linen kerchief
—the original amice—which was bound tightly to the head
with the fillet. Necessity probably dictated this covering of
the head under the fillet, for the tonsure must have left the

priest's head very sensitive to the cold, and all Italy is not "Sunny Italy" by any means.

Next, a cord was passed longitudinally across the scalp, being fastened to the fillet at both ends.

Next, the cord was replaced by a band as broad as the fillet, and a further development trimmed the hanging edges of the kerchief beneath the fillet.

The next inevitable step was to sew fillet and cross-band to the kerchief: to treat the kerchief, in fact, as a hat, reducing fillet and cross-band to mere decorative strips—as soon, with gold embroidery and jewel-work, they became the lappets receiving their share of ornamentation at the same time.

Bishop's mitre, 8th cent.

There is, of course, something very ancient in this business of fastening on the kerchief by a strip of cloth around the temples: it is the standard head-dress of the desert Arab to this day.

A drawing of the 11th century shows the "mitre," developed in this fashion as a round cap, with a band of embroidered material around the end and another fore-and-aft. The hanging "neck cloth" has vanished, but the lappets are much in evidence.

Yet a mitre of two hundred years earlier, of Byzantine provenance, is much further developed on the way to its final —and present—form. Here the linen on both sides of the central ornamented band has been either pulled out with the fingers—"puffed out"—or padded, so as to produce that "bicornute" effect that we noted in considering the amess.

We have here a head-dress which appears to be identical with that of the Jewish priesthood—and why not, seeing that both must have developed in the same way?

This mitre can be seen on other heads than those of ecclesiastics, and was worn by Jew and Christian alike—of all classes—until the 11th century, after which it is reserved for the clergy of both religions.

This old Persian hat needed to be introduced again through a return to the elements: headband over a kerchief, after which logical development would reproduce the ancient form.

The next step is seen clearly in a drawing of the 10th

*Bishop's mitre,
10th cent.*

century, where the "puffed out" parts of the crown on each side of the central band have been pulled out sideways, to stand horizontally over the ears.

The following step was almost the last in the development of the present bishop's mitre: The "puffed out" parts of the crown were pulled *upwards*, in two horns, and stiffened, probably either with cane or wire.

The central band, running across the crown of the head, was retained, but two extra bands, which may have concealed the stiffening cane or wire, were run up the sides of the mitre, from the lower edge to the points of the "horns."

The next, and last, stage is not very easy to account for, though it is curiously paralleled in the custom—observed among early motorists—of wearing the peak of the cap at the back of the head. Or, better still, in the converting of the early 19th century "bicorne" to "fore-and-aft."

*Papal mitre,
15th cent.*

Whatever the reason, early in the 12th century, the two-horned mitre was turned through an angle of 90 degrees, and after that the horns got progressively higher and more pointed —"the mitre increased in height as the wearer acquired greater wisdom," Planché "presumes"—until the 15th century, when the present style was fixed.

By this time, of course, the bishop and his characteristic headwear had become so identified in the public mind that metonymy often used the one indifferently for the other: Barclay, writing in 1514, warns us that "with fork hats it folly is to mell" (i.e., meddle or engage in dispute).

It was Pope Innocent IV who first presented the cardinals with their distinctive hats—distinctive in so far as they were red, and not in that they were wide-brimmed and low-crowned: cardinals had been wearing the ancient Greek *petasos* for centuries before Innocent "first made the hat the symbol or cognizance of the cardinals, injoining them to wear a red hat, at all ceremonies and processions, as a token of their being ready to spill their blood for Christ."

*Cardinal's hat,
no hood, 14th
cent.*

The mitre was made compulsory for bishops and priests in the 11th century; that is to say, it was officially "reserved" to the clergy, and accordingly made no longer permissible for lay wear. It may be that the 90-degree turn of the mitre was because women—who are not to be dictated to in matters of fashion—were wearing horned hats. The steeple—the hennin—and horned hats were not the fashion until the 15th century; but fashions are always anticipated, sometimes by many centuries; a portrait of the Lady Matilda, "great Countess of Tuscany" (1046–1115) shows her wearing a steeple hat over a wimple; and a bas-relief from the tomb of Maria de Molina shows the Queen of Castile wearing a horned head-dress with reticulated caul and wimple. The date of this bas-relief is of the early 14th century, but the horned hat or head-dress for women may have been "in" at the beginning of the 12th century, which is why the bishops chose to wear their horned head-dresses in a novel manner.

Bishop, c. 1110

The cardinal's hat, being derived from the ancient, and secular, wide-brimmed hat which could be slung at the back by cords, needed something to take it out of the ordinary. This was achieved, partly by giving it an unusual (and, in those days, most expensive) colour, and by adding tassels to the cords.

Ecclesiastical heraldry was quick to seize on the possibilities of the multiplicity of the tassels terminating the two cords of the cardinal's hat, and after Innocent IV had granted the red hat to his cardinals in 1245, the heralds began to indicate rank and precedence within the Sacred College by the number of tassels on the hat. The expression, "hat," for a cardinalate has apparently gone out of usage; but the disappearance is only recent. The hat itself went out of all but ritual and symbolic usage five hundred years ago, when, at the latter part of the 15th century, it was replaced, for practical purposes by the biretta. But the hat, which, on reception, covers the cardinal's head once—and once only (being then hung up in his titular church, to stay on the wall until it rots)—remained the traditional symbol of the highest ecclesiastical dignity below that of Pope, and continues to form part of a cardinal's coat-of-arms. The flat hat, with tassels, was not confined to cardinals: only hats of red were. Archbishops and bishops wore green hats; abbots, black.

5—H.H.

Pope's coif, 12th cent.

We have seen that a papal tiara, slightly modified from the Etruscan tiara of the flamen, appears in Christian iconography as early as the end of the 6th century. The triply-crowned tiara of Rome was not, like Rome itself, built in a day; but is the product of centuries—nearly ten of them—of development.

Popes wore the bishop's mitre until the late 15th century; and in earlier times, rank—after popes and lesser clergy had given up the habit of officiating at the divine office bareheaded—was indicated by the colour of the coif or zucchetto (the skull-cap, or coif without strings).

The coif, when first introduced, was considered effeminate—which is possibly why the Church and the Law were the first to adopt it. But, by the 12th century, it had been taken up by all classes, the fabric of which it was made depending upon the rank and/or purse of the wearer. Worn under the crown or hood by persons of rank, it gradually acquired the significance of colour, especially among churchmen.

Among churchmen, too, the strings tying the coif under the chin were early abandoned, and the coif or skull-cap was made to stay firm by cutting it to fit closely to the head.

From the 13th century onwards, the finest caps were made of Batiste, a tightly woven fabric, made of fine linen thread (today's "batiste" is made of cotton), and named after its originator, Batiste of Cambrai, whose home-town has also given a name to a linen fabric.

The skull-cap of the Pope was usually white, but sometimes red; of the cardinals, red; of the bishops, violet; of deans, canons and priests, black.

Sometimes, for "conspicuous services" to the Church, the Popes would present a mitre to the abbots of certain privileged houses, or even laymen. These "honorary" mitres were usually of purple silk, lined with ermine.

White, R. Turner Wilcox points out, had been used, even in the earliest times, to mark the dignity of the prelates of high rank; but he does not add that the Pope dresses in white—with scarlet shoes—because white was the colour of the togas of the Roman Senate, and that he holds that his office inherits the traditional power, not only of the Roman High

Priest—that Pontifex Maximus whose title the Popes have adopted—but of the Roman Senate.

If the evidence of a coloured miniature of Pope Martin V (1417–1431) is to be accepted, the Popes of the later Middle Ages did not invariably wear white. In this miniature the Pope is shown not only habited in "cardinal's red" but wearing a red, triply-crowned tiara.

I have said that the three-crowned tiara took nearly a thousand years to develop.

After the first appearance in Christian art of the "Etruscan" tiara (6th century), the development of the Papal tiara is towards a plain, perfectly regular conical hat—a "dunce's hat," on which Pope Nicholas I (858–867) replaced the jewelled fillet by a crown (what we should now call a ducal coronet). Certain drawings make it clear that some, at least, of these early tiaras were made of unstiffened material, and the point of the "dunce's cap" was adorned with a silken or woollen tuft: possibly having some symbolical affinity with the woollen thread with which the Egyptian soldier, in Graeco-Roman times, used to wind the spike of his two-horned helmet.

Papal tiara, 10th cent.

On the other hand, there is a 10th century representation of a Pope's tiara, which has the bulbous outline of today's shape: this has the jewelled fillet, still, and no crown, and the bulbous surface of the tiara is covered with lines, possibly of raised embroidery, running both horizontally and vertically. If one imagines the skeleton of a Zeppelin, with the end cut off, one will have a very fair mental picture of this 10th century tiara.

Here we may have artist's licence. For the fact is that the crown, with which Nicholas I had replaced the fillet, had not only come to stay: it was to have company.

It is rather significant that the second crown should have been added to the tiara by Alexander III, in the year in which he made his compact with pagan Duke William to "take over" England. If there was any symbolism in the second crown, the symbolism was of a somewhat dubious kind.

The third crown was added by Urban V (1362–1370), who reigned at the beginning of that Hundred Years War which was to establish the balance of power in Europe for six centuries.

Papal tiara, 13th cent.

Two hundred years later, by which time the present bulbous shape had been reintroduced, the "mound with cross" of temporal sovereignty had been added to the apex of the tiara.

There is something very ancient in this symbol, the exact nature of which is easily seen when one reverses it; and that the late Middle Ages were in no doubt of the origin of the tiara, is proved by their name for it—a *phrygium*.

But before we leave this survey of the development of the ecclesiastical head-dress, there is one interesting point to be noted: a cardinal of the 14th century is shown with the brim of his hat turned up all around—the basic form of every hat of the period from 1660 to 1800. All that the cardinal's hat needs is a pinch with the fingers, to give the brim a "cock," and his hat would be anticipating fashion by some four centuries.

Cardinal's hat, upturned brim, over shaped cap, 14th cent.

Perhaps the most extraordinary of all these anticipations is to be found in the shape of a gold crown—French, 13th century— which is worn over a wimple. Obviously the gold crown was based on an original in felt or plaited straw: but, line for line, this golden "hat" of the 13th century is identical with those worn (in velvet) by the ladies of Venice, as may be seen in the paintings of Guardi or of Canaletto. The resemblance is all the more striking, as the Venetian women of the 18th century still retain the wimple, wearing their tricorn hats over it.

Mention of felt recalls that there is some mystery in its origin, as far as Europe is concerned: that the mystery is an old one is shown by the fact that, like fire, and tea-drinking, and metal-working, felt-making had been given a legendary origin as early as the 12th century, when the hatters began to celebrate, each November 23rd, the feast-day of St Clement, "the inventor of felt."

It seems almost certain that the secret of making felt from chopped-up rabbit fur and animal glue was reintroduced from the East, through the Crusaders' contact with the "Saracens," who were skilled felt-makers, using felt both for their large round tents—"yurts"—and for various articles of clothing and horse furniture. Felt-making had been practised in

Europe before the break-up of the Empire: but, apparently it had been neglected, and the secret lost. Somewhere about the time of the first Crusade, felt reappears in Europe, though it was not until 1300 that we hear of any other colour than black. Green was the first colour in use after the traditional black, and only very gradually did the other colours appear. It was the same with velvet, which first appears both at Paris and Venice before 1200, the velvet-weavers of Venice constituting themselves into a trade guild in 1247.

At first plain, and always black, this black velvet began to be patterned in the 14th century. Not until the 15th century do we encounter velvet in colours other than black.

But to return to St Clement, and the tale of how he "discovered" felt.

"Treading upon rabbits" fur to ease his travel-worn feet, he found that the fur became a solid inner sole of felt. . . ."

A curious sort of felt: for, unless the Saint had perspiration of abnormal viscosity, the fur would hardly "mat," and, in any case, it is the mixing of the finely chopped hair with glue which makes felt. But it is only a legend, its importance being that its existence means that the true origin of felt had been forgotten by those who invented the legend.

Chapter Six

VARIOUS HAT STYLES OF THE 15TH AND EARLY 16TH CENTURY

To go back to the beginning of the 15th century: for the first few years, between the end of Richard II's reign and that of the pious, epileptic, cultured and unhappy Henry VI, little change was to be observed in the fashions either of men or of women.

But in the first half of the century, a great change was to take place: men's legs were to be freed. The long gown—the houppelande—was still worn, and would continue to be worn for decades to come. But now the houppelande was tending to be either a ceremonial robe, or, as we should put it, an "overcoat." It covered garments very different in conception: short and tight-fitting—the doublet (surviving until the end of the 17th century, and returning in the late 19th as the "cardigan") and the cote-hardie.

These two garments, which were to form the basis for men's clothing until the introduction of breeches—"Venetians"—in Elizabeth's reign, left the legs entirely free. It is significant that such workmanlike fashions should have been adopted in a century so full of things to be done and things actually accomplished. It shows that the century was aware, even though vaguely, of what was happening.

The hats, too, reflect the change from somewhat indolent fashion to the fashion of active endeavour. The liripiped hood and the liripiped turban are still used, and even plainer forms, such as the "padded roll," have so much dagging that they resemble wreaths of leaves.

The Oriental touch is even more noticeable: but side by side with these fanciful and (one would have thought, especially of four-feet-long liripipes) inconvenient fashions, the simpler ones are surviving and finding more patrons.

For example, the plain padded roll, with a "bag" forming a

Turban hat with liripipe,
c. 1450

70

"crown," was as popular as the "hats" with dagging. We shall meet the hat with the bag-crown later: for, adopted into military use, it was developed into some now historic regimental forms.

Again, the simple forms of regular outline reveal the presence, in production, of hatters as well as milliners (the latter word being used here in the modern sense). In other words, the hat fashions of the developing 15th century, show the moulding of felt as well as the plying of needle to cloth.

Such hats, for example, as that worn by Jan Arnolfini in Jan van Eyck's famous portrait were hats made of the same materials as the modern hatter uses, and constructed in exactly the same way.

For the first time, in the early part of the 15th century, we encounter hats of a modern type: the moulded, brimmed, symmetrical hat, which is not a cap, or hat-cap or anything else but a hat.

*Wide-brimmed fur hat,
c. 1455*

An invoice of this time gives up proof of another survival. It is quoted in Roger's *Agriculture and Prices*: "Fur to Mayor's hat," which proves that the materials, if not the exact shape, of His Worship's hat have not altered in five centuries.

The hatter, indeed, was becoming a man of importance in the list of those who supplied "necessary superfluities"— things with which it is possible to dispense, but which never are gone without.

Writing in the same year, 1431, which gave us the above reference to the fur on the Mayor's hat, Lydgate mentions "Fyne felt hats or spectacles to reede."

We have mentioned that, a little earlier—1412–1413—the Durham MS Almoner's Roll gave this point to the increasing use of hats as hats:

Pro hatbandys de serico negro, ijs.

There is an entry in Ripon Ch. Act. 120, which shows that a standby of modern hatting had been introduced: the entry refers to "Majoria Claton, Cappeknytter."

That knitting had been practised long before 1465, the date of the entry, is evident. The men and women found in the

Jutland bogs wear knitted garments: but there is no direct evidence that knitting was practised in England until the late Middle Ages.

But that hat-making—whether knitting them or moulding them from felt or sewing them up from pieces of cloth—was profitable is evident from an Act of 4 Henry VII ix, 1488–1489, which bitterly complains how "Hatmakers and Kapmakers doth [sic] sell their hattes and cappes at such an outrageous price."

Hat with turned-up brim, Italian, worn over hood, 1505

Now to the 15th century hats themselves: this century saw the disappearance of the hood, despite the fact that, as it was pointed out earlier, the hood with liripipe was being worn (at a funeral) as late as 1585.

The well-known engraving of Albrecht Dürer: *The Conversion of St Eustace*, which may be dated to about 1504, shows the saint wearing a salade, beneath which he wears a buttoned hood which just covers the throat, but does not reach the shoulders, the buttons fastening at the side of the head. Except for children and some old men, however, the hood was out in England fifty years before Dürer executed the engraving of St Eustace.

Before the hood disappeared completely among the young and the fashionable, there is one fashion of wearing it which deserves mention here.

Side by side with the hood with closed gorget and long liripipe, went another, smaller type, with an open gorget buttoning in front. The interesting thing about these small hoods is that they were rarely worn as such, but were slipped back, to form a muffler around the neck. (Incidentally, what a priest of the Benedictine Order does with his black silk hood, before he says mass.)

Naturally, the buttoning—hitherto reserved for women's hoods—provoked unkind comment from those whose self-chosen business it is to criticize anything and everything. The criticism, however, did not affect the run of the fashion. These hoods were apparently sometimes set with gold, silver and precious stones.

Hats continued to sport the liripipe until nearly the end of the century: say until the end of Richard III's reign; and, as the liripipe was dagged from about the time of Agincourt onwards, it is easy to see how it survives, vestigially, as cockade or shoulder-knot.

The head-turban was going out, but the chaperon (in some of its forms not easily distinguished from the hood-turban) was to survive the first three-quarters of the century.

Turban type hood, liripipe over shoulder, c. 1430

The ferment in Europe—political and commercial—was producing new ideas of luxury, which, in turn, fed on the materials designed to satisfy the taste for luxury. Sir John Fastolf's Wardrobe gives indications of the richness of supply of the materials available to the wealthy: "Hood of scarlet, with a roll of purple velvet, bordered with the same velvet"; "Hood of russet velvet, the tippet lined with russet silk"; "Hood of damask russet with tippet fastened with a lace of silk."

Yet, even with the ready-made chaperon, there were different styles, each of which was to play its part in the development of hats of later generations. One form—the simplest —consisted of a roundlet (or padded roll), with gorget (i.e., cock's-comb) and no liripipe. In other styles, the cock's-comb fell over the edge of the roundlet on one side, the liripipe hanging down on the other. Sometimes the cock's-comb was stiffened, so that it stood up above the roundlet like a Japanese paper fan; and sometimes, when there was no liripipe, the limp cock's-comb was allowed to fall over the back of the neck, a fashion which was seen on women's heads in the period immediately at the end of the last Second World War.

Not only ecclesiastics wear a close fitting skull cap, which is cut to fit the head closely, and which comes down far on the nape of the neck, and the coif, though it continues in use, tends to become more and more reserved to the professions, particularly the Law.

Popular during the twenty years ending with Agincourt was an early form of the earlier toppers: a tall, flat-topped hat, having a rolled or closely turned-up brim, so that it looks, in the paintings of the time, like a topper with its brim cut off. There is a tendency to represent the hat as having a forward

"Top hat," c. 1410

or sideways tilt, independent of the wearer's way of putting it on, but this may indicate that the materials of which the hat was made were softer than are used in a modern topper.

There was the hat with a bag-crown, that we have mentioned; this lasted longer than the "topper"; and the "Robin Hood" with the brim turned down in front, was still in use, as it had been from the 11th century. There was a hat with a round crown, which was worn throughout the 15th century, in one or other of two forms: that is, with the large brim turned up, or with the brim either turned down or rolled.

High crowned, early 15th cent.

Popular in the mid-century—say from 1430–1460—was the hat with moderately wide brim and large balloon-shaped crown.

With this hat, the brim was usually turned up slightly in front, as was the case with another hat with a large crown of the so-called hour-glass shape. Both these big hats may be seen, very carefully delineated, in the paintings of Jan van Eyck; one of the most trustworthy sources for fashions of the period (*circa* 1435).

There is also a hat of conical shape, with (often) embroidery spiralling around the crown. The brim of this hat—sometimes faced with fur—is turned up, and a sort of "flourish" has been given to the brim by cutting a little tail on the upper edge.

Yet it must not be thought that the plain hat, of symmetrical outline, easily displaced the elaborate turban-like affairs, with bagged or dagged crowns falling over shoulders or necks.

All the same, simplicity was on its way to triumph. One of the most interesting types of headwear which came in with the 15th century is a cap, with round, flat, deep crown, and brim, often faced with fur, turned closely up. The brim was slit at each side, so that sometimes it was worn—as Dutch fishermen still wear it—with the "back flap" turned down.

Round-brimmed cap, late 15th cent.

This cap with the slit brim was, by the end of the century, to provide a standard type of headgear, which, through the full length of its development, would cover some two centuries of time.

To those who lived at that time, the most important happening was the capture of Constantinople by the Turks in 1453.

A drawing made of Constantine XI a few years before the fall of his ancient capital, shows him wearing a turban, a rope of pearls being twisted spirally around the silk.   That this was an act of defiance—albeit the defiance of a despairing man—seems certain, for it was a crime punishable by death under Mohammedan law, for an infidel to wear the turban. Not merely the green turban, signifying that the wearer had made the journey to Mecca; but any turban.

Byzantine Emperor's cap with turban brim, 1449-1453

Yet the Turks did not kill Constantine—even when they reached Trebizond.   All that they wanted was Byzantium, the city of their age-old dreams.

As has been said, the Turks, when they reached Constantinople, spared city and people, and adopted Greek fashions.

What particularly concerns us here is that having spared Constantinople and its people, the Turks adopted Greek hats both for men and women, but, as the turban was compulsory for Turkish subjects of the Moslem faith, the turban was worn with the Greek pilos, the close fitting cap of leather or felt which had once been worn particularly by the soldiers, sailors and athletes of ancient Greece, but which was now as common a form of headgear as a bowler or a soft felt hat is among us.

This red felt cap—which was to become so distinctively Turkish that Mustafa Kemal Atatürk saw in it the greatest obstacle to the full westernizing of his people, and accordingly abolished it—was nothing but a Greek hat in the beginning.

The curious thing is that the other great Turkish reformer, the Sultan Mahmud, decreed, in the early 19th century, that the turban was no longer obligatory, but that the tarboosh—or fez—must be retained.   Only in 1925 was the red cap, adopted by the Turks in 1453, forbidden.

Incidentally, the tarboosh got its other name, *fez*, from the chief city of Morocco, outside which grew a shrub whose berries yielded a dye supposed to be "the only thing" for dyeing felt the required red colour.

Conservative Egyptian gentlemen still wear the fez, and it had a vogue in England at various times during the last century.

The turban has had such influence on hat-fashions in the West, that a few words must be said about it here.

The English words, *tulip* and *turban* both derive from the one Persian word, *dulband*, a sash. Earlier forms of the word in English are tolibant, tulipant and turbant. It was convenient to differentiate forms, so that one could apply to the flower, the other to the headwrap. In most countries in which the turban is habitually worn, it is, as it were, the vastly exaggerated headband or "puggaree" of a conical felt hat on which the turban is formed. This hat which is retained when the turban is left off, is known as the *taj*, a Persian-Arabic

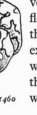

Damask turban, 1460

word meaning crown.

During the centuries in which turbans have been wrapped, there has been time for the development of an elaborate turban-symbolism, with sumptuary laws and tables of precedence, and taboos on shape and material. However, in all this extensive *snobismus*, one thing remains common to all turbans, in all countries: the wrapping must leave the forehead bare, so that, when prostrated at prayer, the worshipper's head may touch the ground.

The ordinary Muslim hat is always unpeaked. Indeed, the Persians have an unpeaked bowler which is named the *kolah*, the echo of sound having caused many people to see, in "kolah," the origin of "bowler." But the laws of philology prohibit such a derivation. In any case, if the "bowler" really owes its name to a hatter, William Bowler, it is still a hat-name which falls into a well-defined class of hat-names; for if, rather than derive "bowler" from "William Bowler," we derive it from "bowl" (an object that the hat resembles), we have a curious and surely not insignificant parallel to the development of the name of a helmet, basinet, from OF *bacinet*, diminutive of *bacin*, a basin.

One word for hat survives from this period, but the word, which once meant "cap," generally, now means a hat of a certain kind. This old word, biggin, derived from the French, *béguin,* which originally meant the head-dress of the Beguine nuns. Palsgrave explains the word: *byggen for a childes heed: beguyne,* and the word survives in the name for the heavy leather hat worn by the Billingsgate fish-porters—a "baggin hat," as they call it.

The great lords of the Middle Ages had, from the beginning of heraldry, dressed their servants and retainers in their livery: the Black Prince, in the mid-14th century, dressed his retainers in black, each man bearing on his chest the cognizance of the white feather that the Black Prince had inherited from his mother, Philippa of Hainault.

The retainers of all the lords wore the "livery" colours, which were the principal two colours of the coat-of-arms; and they wore, usually, some badge as well: a custom much older than the wearing of the "livery" colours, since the retainers of the Roman emperors wore a badge on their left shoulder.

But it was left to a man who destroyed the power of the great nobles—and who began by an attack on their custom of keeping private armies—not only to establish the first permanent military body in Britain since the departure of the legions, but to be first to put the royal retainers into what was, in effect, uniform dress.

"The Yeomen of the Guard of Our Lord the King," established by Henry VII immediately after he had seized the throne, was made up of men who had formed Henry's bodyguard at Bosworth. The dress that this corps wears today is more deliberately archaic than the survival of early Tudor dress, but, except for the fact that the first Yeomen of the Guard wore Tudor green-and-white, and not the present scarlet, the uniforms that the "Beefeaters" wear, gives one a fair picture of what the men looked like who accompanied the miser Tudor on his plundering expeditions from great house to great house.

Before we go on to examine the men's hat fashions as the 15th century drew to its close, let us see what was happening to women's heads.

As the 14th century gave way to the 15th, the horned head-dress made its appearance: its introduction is generally credited to Isabel of Bavaria (1371–1435), a lady whose curious tastes in other directions caught the fancy of that connoisseur of the odd, the Count de Sade.

All the same, the two-horned head-dress had been seen at intervals during the three preceding centuries, and its genesis, anyway, is inherent in the head-dress consisting of a veil draped over boldly projecting templers. The "horns" were made by draping the veil over a wire frame; but until the triumph of both the double- and single-horned head-dress, vigorous competition was offered by the other types of head-dress, notably by the padded roll.

Veil over wired frame, hair in templars, c. 1410

The padded roll, in fact, was never completely displaced by the one- and two-horned head-dress. By turning the two sides of the roll up, until they nearly joined, and by "filling in the sides," a sort of two-horned head-dress was devised which is highly characteristic of the century. This belongs to the very middle of the century, as does another head-dress of singular type: the turban head-dress to which the plaits of the wearer's hair are fastened in a symmetrical way.

Earlier in the century, one finds "the lot": horned head-dress with wired-up veil, worn over huge templers, and surmounted by a coronet. As the century wore on, women's fashions tended towards lightening the burden on the head: the head-dresses towered up, higher and higher, but the materials used were of the lightest; mostly wire and gauze or muslin.

The two-horned head-dress was commonly called the "escoffion," and the single-horned, the so-called "steeple hat," was called the "hennin," supposedly from the Flemish, *hennen*, a cock, though the derivation seems a little strained to me.

With the steeple-like hennin went the starched linen or muslin wings kept erect on a wire frame; but the hennin could sometimes be worn without this tricking out by starched material. Nor had the hennin always to end in a sharp point: often the hennin was truncated, and a very plain—and most becoming—version of the hennin was the so-called "chimney pot" head-dress, with the narrow veil passing over the top of the hennin and around the chin. This was a true hat, and not a mere "head-dress."

Hennin head-dress, c. 1460

As the century grew older, the extravagance of women's head-fashions provoked the inevitable reaction, and from excessive elaboration they turned to a somewhat self-conscious simplicity.

There were those who stuck to the steeple hats, with multiplicity of veiling and it must be remarked that, despite a Court ordinance of 1507, the women of the 15th century had already begun to abandon wimple and barbette, and showed neck and bosom as well as something of their arms. But many women, towards the end of the century, left off the hat, steeple or chimney-pot, and adopted the Continental fashion of draping the head in stiffened, transparent veiling.

The "sausage-shaped" roll, with either a deep V or an equally deep U over the forehead, continued to be worn up to the end of Richard III's reign, but the U shape was covered with a thick veil.

The turban remained fashionable, growing in size, until it went out at about the same time as the sausage-shaped roll disappeared.

High-crowned head-dress, veil under chin, 15th cent.

An interesting head-dress, which again was a true hat, was the high-crowned bonnet, whose wide brim was turned up in front, so that the sides framed the face as they fell sharply away to the shoulders. The shape of the crown showed considerable variation; but the sharp up-turn of the brim, with the falling away of the sides, established a type of hat which is still with us: the Summer Girl Hat. The hat was popular from about 1460 to the accession of Henry VII, a happening which is reflected very noticeably in fashions: many a fashion dying, and many a fashion coming in, as Richard III died and Henry Tudor became king.

Among the fashions which went with the coming of the Tudors was a head-dress which, to us, seems most characteristic of the whole second half of the 15th century: the "Butterfly" head-dress, which was built upon a fez-like cap, worn well at the back of the head. The cap supported a wire frame which was covered with a diaphanous veil, arranged in the usual two-horned manner, so as to give the impression of a pair of wings.

With the coming of the new king, fashions underwent a complete change, and though older people still kept to the styles of earlier days, the fashionable men and women adopted new modes of covering the head. The high-crowned hood and the butterfly head-dress survived the coming of Henry Tudor, but not the end of the century: by 1495, even the most traditional had abandoned these, for the head-dress from which was to develop the "Gable" head-dress of the next century.

Earliest version of "the English hood," late 15th cent.

Something of the classical hatred of excess affected the fashions of the time: hats for men, in England and northern Europe (Germany excepted) at least; and the simple caul came back for women: a fashion which was to return in Charles I's reign, and again in the 1830s.

The style of head-dress from which the Gable was to develop in the next century consisted in stiffening the edges of the veil to form a hood with vertical edges framing the face, the unstiffened part of the hood falling over the crown and back of the head, the ends being brought forward over the shoulders. The stiffened edges of the hood were lined with some brightly contrasting colour, and as the edges of the hood stood away from the face sufficiently to reveal a tightly fitting linen or velvet coif (itself often edged with jewel-set embroidery), the "New Look" of the Tudor Woman had, it will be seen, arrived.

The straight edge across the forehead had only to be bent into an angle—a "gable"—and the next stage in the fashion-development of the Tudor mode was achieved.

The "Gable hood," c. 1500

For men, this was an age—Bosworth onwards—in which a strange uniformity descended, as it does at intervals through history. The small hat was "in," and though the Continent, especially in Italy and Germany, held out for a long time against the minimizing trend of fashion, notably with regard to hats and caps, they too succumbed in the end. By 1600, both Italians and Germans had been converted to the almost general use of the small hat—just as the small hat was about to be displaced by the large "King Charles" or "Laughing Cavalier" hats of the early 17th century.

As the 15th century drew to a close, England, France and the Netherlands had adopted the small hat for men, which was eventually to be the general masculine headwear for Europe until about 1600.

"Gable hood," c. 1500

The women, abandoning the other types of headgear, were taking—again almost as a body—to the veil-with-stiffened edges, worn over the caul, which had been reintroduced to "complete" the new hood-veil.

Italy, in the latter half of the 15th century, showed some curious styles, especially on men's heads—but just how far may we trust Uccello, Pisanello, Piero della Francesca, Carpaccio and other great decorative artists? If we may trust them as faithful recorders of unusual fashions, then we may accept the fact that one of Uccello's models wore a crimson damask "mob cap" of the sort recently seen for a short period on the heads of our more fashion-conscious young women. A Pisanello knight is wearing a straw hat as wide as that of Chaucer's Wife of Bath; and a man in a Piero della Francesca painting wears a tall hat like an inverted lampshade, fitting tightly to the crown of the head and flaring outwards as it rises.

Straw hat, c. 1460

Indeed, Italian art gives us every variation on style, so far as men's hats and caps go. There are hats plain and elaborately dagged and copiously liripiped; there are hats small, and hats large, hats with brims and hats without. One of Piero della Francesca's knights wears a helmet exactly like the cap as worn by a modern jockey, and even more startlingly anticipatory is the same cap, seen in a Flemish illuminated MS, with the peak turned sharply upwards, so that the man pictured looks for all the world as though he is wearing a U.S. Army fatigue cap.

Everything, in fact, is anticipated, even the "Puritan" (later "Byronic") collar can be seen in a painting of Antonio del Pollaiuolo, of date 1469.

Cap with turned-up peak, c. 1460

Among all the flamboyant head-dresses, there are found the master-types of the plainer sort, from which the small hats and caps of the 16th century were to develop, and which, development arrested by tradition, were to provide the legal

6—H.H.

and ecclesiastical head-dresses for a dozen justiciaries and as many Faiths.

Italian judge's high hat, worn over hood, c. 1450

It may not be unreasonable to suggest that the small hat came in after Bosworth—or, rather, the small hat drove out the large hat after Bosworth—because, though not everyone was embarking on voyages for the New World, there was considerable movement; and just as civilians wear military fashions at the time of a popular war, so, I think, did men wear the garb of action: the short tunic, the small hat.

As the century turned into a new one, the small hat became established for another reason. It had been adopted by Church and Law (and, until the Reformation, they were mostly the same). One is often struck by the "clerical" appearance of the great disputants of the time: even where the wearers of the biretta-like and slit-brimmed hats are not clergymen, they look like it, so intimately have we come to identify certain types of headgear with the professions which made them peculiarly their own trademark.

Traveller's cap, c. 1425

The person in Holbein's famous picture of *The Ambassadors* is the very archetype of the ecclesiastically-typed civilian. He is a diplomat, but it is hard, seeing not only his biretta, long, plain, wrap-over gown, and "dog collar," not to take him for a cleric of some kind.

The resemblance between the headgear of civilians and those of clergy and lawyers was probably not accidental: in all the bickerings which went on about God and ecclesiastical discipline and—which was more to the point—about ecclesiastical wealth, all the really earnest arguers, if not clergymen, thought of themselves as well within the charmed circle of ecclesiastical privilege.

Kings were priests, anyway: the Kings of France thought so (which is why the King of France, upon being crowned, always assumed the titular government of a monastery), and the Tudors were prepared to think so, too.

Velvet cap, worn over hood, late 15th cent.

Henry VII wore the close fitting black cap, with closely turned-up brim, slit at each side; but Henry VIII, his son, did not. If a portrait discovered by a Hexham railway-porter connoisseur some thirty years ago is a genuine Clouet portrait of Henry VIII, then the flat hat always associated with the king and his son was adopted by Henry VIII very early in life.   He made it his own, just as, in later times, Queen Mary was to make the toque her own.

The 16th century began with the small hat, generally called a bonnet, dominating all others as the favourite headgear for men.

This most characteristic hat of the first half of the 16th century is seen in its original form in the well-known portraits of Edward IV, Richard III and Henry VII.   Essentially a hat of a "pork-pie" nature, with a close-fitting, up-turned brim, the practice of slitting the brim vertically, often with more than one slit, produced forms which were to turn up again in British Army uniform in the mid-18th century.   There is a hat, seen on a figure in a tapestry woven about 1510 (Flemish), which is identical with a hat worn by a Guards' officer in 1756. This, by the way, was the early 16th century hat of the somewhat larger kind.

Round cap, c. 1460

These hats, however, as far as England and France were concerned, were never as popular as the small ones, which were worn indoors as well as out, and, generally speaking, from 1500 to 1545, they tended to remain low and soft in the crown, the whole hat getting flatter as the 16th century proceeded.

One hat-fashion should be mentioned here: the habit of wearing either gold or silver tags (*aglets*) or a "jewel" in the hat.

This was a custom of decided antiquity, which was revived about the middle of the 15th century, and spread all over the West.

The last notable man to conform to this extravagance was Lord Nelson, whose life was lost to him as a consequence of his wearing the diamond-studded "Plume of Feathers," the *Chelink*, presented to Nelson by the Sultan of Turkey.   Part of the *Chelink* turned by clockwork, and a French marksman, seeing the diamonds coruscating in an enemy hat, had no doubt of the importance of the hat's wearer.

In the famous autobiography of Benvenuto Cellini, we read that "it was the custom at the time, that men's bonnets were

Small cap, Italian, late 15th cent.

trimmed in front or over the temple with a jewel, brooch or medallion.

"It was the custom at this epoch to wear little golden medals upon which every nobleman or man of quality had some device or fancy of his own engraved, and these were worn in the cap."

A bequest in a York Will, 1508–1509, is quoted by the Cunningtons: "My scarlet bonnet w^t a trew-love (quatrefoil) of silver and gilt apone it."

Dame Agnes Humphries's inventory, 1523, gives us a price:

"A bonnet of black velvet and a brooch on it, cost 5 marks" —an expensive hat: £3 6s. 8d., of which the shillings and pence would buy the hat itself; £3 being thus the cost of the brooch.

As for aglets, these seem to have been favoured by the elegant youth: his seniors preferring jewel or brooch or medallion.

"A goodly youth," says Spenser, in *The Faerie Quene*, "wearing an hood with aglets spread."

The development of the smaller hat can be summarized as follows:

Cap with slashed brim, c. 1510

By 1500, men were wearing bonnets having a small crown, with close-fitting, vertically turned-up brim, which might have two (one at each side) or more slits cut in it.

Within five years from this date, we find that the crown has grown fuller and softer, and thus flatter, forming what one historian of costume has noted as a "tam o' shanter" effect. The brim, too, has undergone some change: it is now wider, and saucer-shaped.

Another five years—the date being now 1510—crowns are as wide or even wider, the fashion being to tab the brim or twist it in extravagant manner.

By 1520, the crowns are much flatter, though the brim is still turned up.

From 1530 onwards, until about 1560, the hat diminished in size, tending to be thrust back until it perched on the crown of the head. The crown of the hat itself was flat, the small, untabbed brim being either flat or drooping.

With regard to the hat of intrinsically larger proportions, this—over the period that we are now considering—appeared in two main types. One was a plain hat, with large crown and wide brim: it was worn by country folk and travellers, but tends to become increasingly rare after about 1515. The other was a large hat with a low crown, a spreading, bowl-shaped, upturned brim, worn at the back of the head. It was often trimmed with a plume of ostrich-feather, and was generally worn with an undercap.

This type of hat was generally supplied with strings, either for tying under the chin, or to enable the hat to be slung over the back of the shoulder.

Strings were also used to tie the flaps of the brim up; the strings being tied over the crown of the hat; though there are representations of hats in which the strings go from the top of the crown to the edges of the brim, using a system seen to this day in the top-hats worn by senior ecclesiastics of the Church of England.

Here I must join issue with those authorities on Dress, the Cunningtons, over their remark that the coif disappeared at the end of the 15th century, save for elderly people, and the professions. Certainly the coif *with strings*—the "baby's bonnet"—went out of general use before 1500, but the under-cap, the coif without strings, continued to be fashionable up to the middle of the 16th century, and continued in use for more than a century after 1550. An engraving of Richard Busby, Master of Westminster School (1640–1695), shows that terror of small boys wearing a wide-brimmed, high-crowned hat over a closely fitting black undercap.

Except for the feather and the jewel, trimming, until about 1545, was comparatively simple. Where fancy needed expression, this expression was achieved by slitting ("castel-lating") the brim, or by giving it some individual twist, as many men do today with the brims of their "soft felts."

Since the cap or bonnet acquired such currency; lasting, with slight changes, until the end of Elizabeth I's reign; some variants on the types already mentioned may be noted here.

An early—*circa* 1480—type had the close-fitting, upturned brim cut away in front, so that the rest of the brim, fitting

Cap, with brim cut away in front, early 16th cent.

snugly around the soft crown, formed, as it were "side flaps" and "back flap" and sometimes these were turned down.

Always with the crown flat, round and shallow, or with a deeper crown having a softer top, the brim of the earlier types of cap was frequently moulded into lobes, exactly as may be seen worn today by Thibetan ecclesiastics.

Buttoned cap, late 15th cent.

The Buttoned Cap was popular from about 1520 until well on into the following century; and though never worn by the fashion-conscious, was most popular especially with countrymen, so that it came to be particularly associated with them. Its period of greatest popularity extended over the thirty years from 1520–1530.

With the Buttoned Cap, the crown was sometimes round and sometimes square, deeper than formerly, and often beret-shaped.

The brim was cut away in front, making the rest of the brim into two side flaps, which could be turned down, to cover the ears, or turned up, and secured either with a button on the crown, or by tapes. We have noted a cap of this type already: the Buttoned Cap differed from it in no very marked particular, save that its shape marked it out as provincial or rural. Just so, today, it would be hard, short of making a drawing of both, to explain the difference between a bowler from the "wrong" shop, and one from the "right" shop. The Buttoned Cap, we may say, always came from the "wrong" shop.

Buttoned cap, early 16th cent.

This type of cap has survived until our own day, both for civilian and military wear. The difference between the modern "Buttoned Cap" and the 16th century type is that, in the modern type, the flat, round crown projects more over the upturned brim, and the modern cap is supplied with a peak. But the "brim" which can be turned down to cover the ears was greatly favoured by early motorists, the "brim" being tied up, when not in use, by strings across the crown. The men of several units during the First World War were supplied with a cap having a "back flap" which could be let down; the flaps were joined by two perforated strips of cloth, fastening with a buckle; sometimes the buckle was fastened in front, sometimes over the cap's top. The button which tops many caps, especially those made in the United States of America, has an aesthetic purpose, in that it hides the point at which the sections of cloth meet, but that it is also a relic of the old Buttoned Cap there can be little doubt.

Flat cap, early 16th cent.

Very popular by 1520, and having a fashionable life which extended over the period, 1505–1545, was the so-called Milan Bonnet. It was, in effect, a soft, full crown, pleated into a headband over a brim which was wide and well turned up. It was slit at each side to form a "front" and "back," the slits sometimes being joined by aglets. The back was generally supplied with tapes, for tying over the crown.

Fashion dictates, at times, a "calculated informality" and readers may remember a fashion among young men, round about 1924, which dictated the wearing of the coat collar turned up; in 1540, or thereabouts, it became fashionable to wear the Milan Bonnet with the "back" always turned down, so that the strings for tying disappeared at this time.

Flat cap, early 16th cent

The Germans introduced the slashed brim, and the elaborate styles of the German hats at this period has already been noted. It was not only among the German Landsknechts that the slashed and slitted hat, with its "crenellated" brim curling inwards, and topped with as many feathers as a Cockney donah of the late 19th century, was popular: other, more pacific, Germans wore them, too.

But in Germany, these hats were much more of a part of the general effect: they were meant to go with suits slashed and puffed to match.

The so-called Halo Hat—a hat in which the turned-up, fairly wide brim hid the crown—was often worn over a caul, and the hat itself was tilted, "cocked," at such an angle as to place the hat well on the side or back of the head.

Obviously there must have been subtle differences in cut and colour and cock and trimming which distinguished the really stylish from the ordinary; the ordinary from the dowdy. The existing pictures of the royal and the noble might be expected to yield much evidence on this point. Looking through any illustrated journal of today, it will be seen that, generally, the world's leaders, or its richest, are hardly ever

Milanese bonnet, early 16th cent.

the best-dressed, for all that they may frequent expensive tailors. Again, the conscious or unconscious tastes of the artist may destroy much evidence: if the artist has no "dress sense," he will make a Brummel or a D'Orsay look provincial; if, like some of our modern fashion-artists, he draws only what he wishes to see, then all his portraits look like fashion-plates. Only rarely do we get the sort of comment which enables us to know that such-and-such a colour or shape is "right," and that such-and-such a tint or line is "wrong."

Such a remark, for instance, as this, *temp.* Edward IV: "tall black bonnets—most genteel."

Few such remarks have been preserved as we proceed, and it is interesting to note that whatever trivia the diarist records, he never thinks of recording, from day to day, the subtle and minute changes in fashion. The catalogues and fashion-plates of tailors and hatters are, even to this day, notorious as being inaccurate guides to what the well-dressed gentleman is wearing.

Again, there are obscurities in old records. Take the word, *cap.* From this ordinance of 36 Henry VIII, it is clear that the "cap" referred to is a cloth bag, probably with a neck gathered on a string:

> Every man to have a cap to be made to
> put his salette ("battle bowler") in,
> after such fashion as I have desired,
> which William Taylor capper doth make
> for me, where you may have as many of
> them as you list for 8d a piece.

Certainly this "cap" was a bag in which the steel helmet might be carried—but might it not have served the purpose of a cap as well, especially a cap to be worn under the salette that it carried? During the last two wars, the British Army authorities issued a "muffler," with instructions that, if one end of the "muffler" be tucked into the other, the soldier would have a warm hat to wear.

Apart from the more extravagantly shaped and trimmed caps, there was a cap of plain, severely practical form that I

Man's cap,
c. 1935

saw only yesterday: the first time, in a Parliament-street haberdasher's window, where it was labelled, *The MacQueen Caphat*, the second in a Cecil-court printseller's window, where it was on the head of Philip Melanchthon, in a 1792 stipple-engraving reproduction of the famous Holbein pencil-drawing in the Royal Collection at Windsor. Indeed, except that Melanchthon has a small piece of cloth sticking out from under the back of his cap, he might well be modelling The MacQueen Caphat, which is a cap made of moulded felt, and not, as with most caps today, made of segments of cloth, canvas or suede leather, stitched together.

To the historian of hats (or even to the historian *tout simple*) a walk around the "popular" hat-shops is instructive. Under such ear-catching trade-names as *Slim Jim, The Broadway, Black Bottom, The Mambo, The Duke of Windsor*, and so forth, the hats that I have seen over the years have reproduced faithfully many of the styles familiar to us from the great portraits of antiquity. Many of the smaller hats of today can be seen, not only in the Italian portraits of the late 15th century, but also in the Dutch paintings of the 17th century. Mac-Queen's Caphat must have been popular: it was, at any rate, with many of Holbein's distinguished sitters, for Brian Tuke is also wearing one—though, being Chancellor of the Exchequer, and no mere philosopher, his is larger than Melanchthon's.

The flat cap, when displaced among the fashionable by the Elizabethan "topper;" originally from Spain, through France; became the mark of citizens and apprentices, and got for itself the name, *City Flat Cap*.

So much did it become the sign of the apprentices—by about 1570—that the apprentices called themselves "flat caps," and the cry, "Flat Caps!" was a rallying-call for the apprentices to organize one of those riots for which they were notorious in the 16th and 17th centuries.

The other plainer forms of cap continued to be worn: the beret and the biretta; and the linen coif, in its full form and in its tapeless form, was used, though the former only by lawyers and other professional men, all careful to tie the tapes under their chin.

Others wore the coif in black cloth, silk or velvet; it was particularly favoured by elderly men, and whether tied under the chin or not was not considered a head-covering of a nature to be removed, even in the presence of royalty.

Writing in the last years of the Commonwealth—more than a century after the period under review, it is observed; "We hold the head uncovered if the hat be off, though the cap be on."

At the beginning of the 16th century, men, as well as women, wore the caul, a close-fitting round cap, worn far back on the head, skull-cap fashion. Made of some richly embroidered material such as silk or velvet, it could be, like the women's cauls, a netted affair of ornamental thread.

The "nightcaps" of the period are not to be confused with the "nightcaps" of later times. The early 16th century nightcap was a close-fitting round cap, often with a turned-up brim, made of velvet or silk and often embroidered. It was made to be worn in the house at night, not in bed.

Flat cap, 1540

A wardrobe inventory of Henry VIII has: "A nightcappe of blacke velvett embroidered."

There were "night caps," of course, in the modern sense of the word. It was only in the late 19th century that people stopped going to bed wrapped up like cocoons: sleeping suits, bed-socks, bed-robes, night caps; and then, deep in the clammy, suffocating embrace of a feather mattress, under mountainous piles of blankets and quilts, go to sleep within the airless box formed by the tester and curtains of their beds.

It is of this other sort of night cap that Andrew Boorde is talking when, in his *First Boke of the Introduction of Knowledge* (1547), he counsels: "Let your nyght cap be of skarlet . . . and in your beed lye not to late, not to colde but in temperance."

Hat materials used were the usual "expensive" staples: silk, satin, velvet, sarcenet. Damask and straw, woollen cloth and felt were also used, as with us. Beaver had been continued over from the previous century, but went out of fashion within the first ten years of the 16th century, not to return to fashion again until the last decade of the same century, after which it remained in use as a staple of the hatter's trade until the second half of the 19th century.

As for women's headgear in the 16th century, it underwent changes as fundamental as those affecting the hats and caps of the men, though, as with the men's headgear, the change came a little before the end of the 15th century coinciding more or less with the accession of Henry VII.

As with men's hats and caps, women's head-dresses tended to become smaller. The hennin and the escoffion—"steeple" and "horned" head-dresses—went out, to be replaced, among the fashionable by the hood that we have mentioned: the hood-veil with a stiffened forward edge, and a veil, or "curtain," covering the back of the head.

But there was another, simpler type of head-covering which came in with the abandonment of the fantastic headgear of pre-Henry VII days: the draped hood, with embroidered forward "face-framing" edge. This was always worn over an undercap usually made of linen, and the "curtain" of the hood was divided at the back, the slit being "caught" by means of a clock such as is still sometimes seen on men's socks.

Dividing the "curtain" up into two "lappets" enabled much variation to be effected in the general appearance of the hood: the lappets could be pinned up in many ways, or they could be brought over the shoulders, to hang down on each side of the bosom. Often the hood was provided with a decorative lining, and the sides of the hood framing the face were bent back, in the manner of the still-worn Dutch girls' caps, to show the contrast of the lining colour.

Turning back the sides of the hood usually revealed either the undercap or the hair—or both. Following the general trend of 16th century fashion, at least as far as headgear was concerned, lappets and curtains were progressively shortened until, by 1520, the draped hood had become something almost as small as coif or caul, but distinguished from either by having "cheek-pieces" which had developed from the turned back sides of the original hood.

A parallel development of the plain linen hood which was fashionable from 1500, but lasting some fifteen years (i.e., to

about 1545) longer than the draped hood, brought the final forms of both to something similar.

The plain linen hood was stiffened to form an arch around the face, with a slight dip over the forehead just where the keystone of an arch in building is found. The V-shaped slit at the back was present, but the lappets of the curtain, instead of being draped over the shoulders, were turned up, and pinned to the head in various ways. The Cunningtons differentiate between the draped hood and the plain linen hood, but the difference is rather one of a mode of arrangement than a difference in basic design.

Plain veil-hood, c. 1530

The plain linen hood developed into the well-known *Mary Stuart* hood, and in its earlier form was a favourite with elderly women or widows, who, by the custom of the time, were forced to regard themselves as having lost their youth. The elderly and widows usually wore with their hoods a barbe or a wimple. The barbe was a bib made of white linen which was pleated on to a tape, whose ends served to tie the barbe around the chin. The lower edge of the barbe reached to the lower edges of the hood. The wimple served the same purpose of concealing the neck, but was plain, not pleated. It was carried around the chin with the ends pinned either to the hair or to the undercap. The wimple was also known as the gorgette.

The Tudors were much addicted to sumptuary laws, and in 1517 the barbe came under Henry VIII's official notice. In an order issued in that year, it was decreed that "duchesses and countesses and all higher estates may be barbed above the chin, everyone not being under the degree of a baroness may wear a barbe about the chin; and all other gentlewomen beneath the throatgoyll (*gullet*)."

"French hood," 1530

We come now to the "English Hood," developed into its characteristic shape, from the stiff-edged hood, by having the part over the forehead bent into an upwards pointing angle, whence its descriptive name of "Gable Hood."

The domination of this type of hood, whose essential feature was its "arch," lasted for a full forty years, from 1500 to 1540, and the conservative and the unfashionable continued to wear it for twenty years after the later date. The "gable" was maintained by wire or other stiffening.

In its earlier form, the English Hood had a curtain at the back, hanging in loose folds, while the two panels framing the face were continued in long lappets, usually embroidered. Another wide band of embroidery was laid across the "roof" of the "gable," and carried down the lappets, or "chaffers."

But, from about 1525 onwards, the English Hood began to be affected by the trend towards economy of bulk which was affecting all headgear. The "framework" of the hood became more rigid, and the lappets were pinned up to the top of the hood. When this was done, the neck and shoulders were no longer hidden, except where the undercap was fastened under the chin.

An undercap, usually of white linen, always being worn with the hood, the edges of the hood could stand well away from the head without exposing the hair; but often the hair, parted in the middle, was visible beneath the edge of the undercap.

The *fouriaux* that we encountered in the 12th century, came back into fashion about 1525. The hair was divided into two plaits and encased in striped *fouriaux*; the two plaits were then brought across the forehead, showing beneath the "gable" of the hood.

"Gable hood," later version, c. 1525

The candy-stripe effect produced by the crossing of the *fouriaux* over the forehead is one which is characteristic of the fashion of this time. Sometimes the plaits were "whipped" with riband; but the effect was the same as that created by the *fouriaux*: the expanse of forehead beneath the "gable" was now filled in with silk-sheathed hair.

The French expedition of Henry VIII, followed by the meeting on the Field of the Cloth of Gold had strengthened French influence on English fashions. And by 1530, the French Hood had come as a rival to the English Hood which it eventually supplanted. The French Hood was small, made on a stiffened foundation, and was always worn far back on the head. The edge of the hood fitted tightly to the head, and the sides were brought forward to end over the ears, leaving the hair exposed above. The back of the crown was raised in a horseshoe curve over the head. The curtain, usually of a dark material, was either arranged in pleats, or was merely a broad flap falling to the shoulders. Sometimes this flap was stiffened and brought up to lie on the top of the head in such a way that the lower edge of the flap projected a little way beyond the face. This was supposed to give protection from the sun, and arranged in this fashion, the hood was known as a "bongrace"—which could also be a separate form of headgear.

We have seen an earlier type of bongrace: the loop of velvet across the forehead. The 16th century bongrace was a sort of sun-hat. It was a rectangular "board" made of stiffened velvet and was worn flat on the head in such a way as to project beyond the face, while the rest of it hung down behind. It could be worn with a hood or a coif, but often it was worn by itself.

*The
"French hood,"
c. 1530*

The French Hood did not remain long unaltered in England. Whereas in the French mode of wearing it the front border was curved, in the English mode it was straight, the crown being flattened so that the hood was wider than the face, the sides of the hood then being curved in to end above the ears. This type of French Hood is always associated with the tragic Queen of Scots. Where an undercap was worn with the French Hood it was never visible. The hood was usually fastened by a band, white or dark, under the chin.

Some of the older forms of hair covering remained in use: the Cornet, originally a pointed hood, whence the name, but which, by the beginning of the 16th century, had developed the point of the hood into a sort of short liripipe which hung down.

Actually, it was almost identical with the bongrace, the difference between cornet and bongrace being small, and so Cotgrave, writing in 1611, makes no distinction between the two: "Cornet, a fashion of shadow or Boongrace used in old time, and to this day by some old women."

It is, in fact, worn to this day by some Italian peasant women.

The French Hood was not costly, though extravagant women could run up the price if they wished. Cunnington quotes the Lestrange Accounts, 1533: "For a French Hood 1s. 3d. 2 velvet cornets for my lady 10d."

The hood was not always plain: bad taste had to adorn this simple elegance. Decorative borders known as "billiments" were added to the borders of the hood. These billiments were made of lined silk tricked out with precious stones or goldsmith's work. Sometimes the jewelled or embroidered border of lawn, velvet or lace was mounted on thin pasteboard, when it was known as a "paste." Brides often wore the "paste" by itself, though it was generally employed as a decorative border for French Hoods.

"French hood," English version, worn with billiments, 1540

It has been stated that hats for women did not come in until the reign of Elizabeth I, but this statement needs some explanation; and if the difference between "cap" and "hat" be held to be no difference at all, then the statement cannot stand.

However, hats did not appear until Elizabeth's reign; but the various types of cap that we noted a few pages back were all adopted by women at this period, being worn over undercaps or coifs. Women adopted the Halo bonnet, the Flat cap and a brimless beret, of the sort seen on the heads of modern British soldiers.

Halo hat, fur-trimmed, over hood, early 16th cent.

This wearing of men's hats reminds me that, even after the end of the First World War, the working women of London's East End had a non-Sunday uniform which consisted of neckless blouse, plain skirt, apron and a man's tweed cap, secured to their tightly-drawn-back hair by a couple of hat-pins. The interesting thing about the way in which these caps were worn was that they were never put on the head as the husbands put them on, but taken just as they had come from the hat-shop—that is to say, perfectly flat—and laid on the top of the head.

Just so the women of the 16th century, adopting men's hats, wore them straight, without any tilt or cock.

Cunnington, remarking upon the fact that the coif or undercap was always worn with a man's cap, notes a curious exception in the Eastern Counties and near Cambridge, from the 1520s to the 1530s. In those parts, the "beret" was worn by women without either coif or undercap.

Another cap worn by women from 1500 to 1580, but with its "fashion-peak" between 1520 and 1545, was the Lettice Cap, made from lettice, a fur resembling that of ermine. The Lettice Cap was marked by a cut of its own: fitting the head closely, and having two "ear flaps" which projected to cover the lower part of the cheeks to the chin, the crown of the cap was raised in a sort of "gable;" the "gable" projecting at each side in points.

Lettice cap,
large type, 1550

Its resemblance to a biretta was angrily remarked by the Puritan, Stubbes, who complained in his *Anatomie of Abuses* that "Some weare lattice cappes with three hornes, three corners I should say, like the forked cappes of Popish priests." It is interesting to note that the *Anatomie of Abuses* was published in 1583, which shows that some diehards were yet wearing this distinctive type of cap.

Half of the 16th century passes, and another great change in fashion is apparent. It was "a great change," because in those times, the changes, occurring less frequently, were more striking. Today, with fashion changing its modes from lustrum to lustrum, we hardly see the change.

Lettice cap,
smaller version,
worn over hood,
1550

But, to the observers of the time, the changes were striking enough. "They show," says Thomas Nash, speaking of his fashionable contemporaries, "the swellings of theyr mind in the swellings and plumping out of theyr apparayle"—but to us the "swellings" seem modest enough.

It may well be that the objection to the mode of the second half of the 16th century had a politico-racial bias, in so much as the change in fashion was directly attributable to foreign influences. To us it seems that the "swellings" that the hearty poets of the latter part of the 16th century found so objectionable were a move, not in the direction of extravagance, but rather the reverse. To us, the change from the "cad's" flat cap to the "topper" of even such aggressive bounders as Francis Drake is a change for the better: not unreasonably, because the "topper" is identified, in our day, with wealth (or the pretension to wealth) and the cap is identified with something lesser.

Two great fashion-changes are to be observed in the latter part of the 16th century: the adoption of breeches ("Venetians") and the alteration of the hat from a fairly wide-brimmed, soft-crowned object, to a narrow-brimmed, tall (yet still small) "topper."

The tall, small-brimmed hat came to us from Spain, but its impact was made the more immediate by the fact of Queen Mary's marriage to Philip of Spain. Whatever the patriotic Englishmen thought of the Queen's Spanish husband, he was converted to the elegance of the Spanish King's entourage: for, no matter what the English have had to say since about the Spaniards, the Spaniard is a man of restrained and calculated elegance. The "stolid" German it is who has fathered some of the world's worst sartorial extravagances.

Boy's high hat, peak at side, 1564

With the Spaniards came the neat, smooth outline; the trim neckline and the small, tall hat.

People like Nash seem to have mistaken the apparel for the man: seeing the latter in the former. What we see is the superb self-confidence of the Elizabethans; and we think we see it—as Nash obviously saw it—in their clothes.

A change that we must also notice is that the men covered their necks (as the men of Henry VIII's time had not done) and the women uncovered theirs. *The Black Book of Arundell*, dealing with Queen Elizabeth's coronation, lays it down that "a quene of England shall go veiled," from the waterside at the Tower to Charing Cross, and so, along 1380 yards of blue cloth, barefoot, to the West door of Westminster Abbey. But the women of Elizabeth's day, and the Queen herself, for that matter, showed neck and bosom. Only the elderly, the diehard and what the French call the *recidiviste* well-bred kept to the neck-covering customs: the veil, the wimple, the barbette, the gorgette.

Top hat, man's, 1580

To split the fashions of the 16th century at the mid-time is inaccurate. Mary came to the throne in 1553, and though she reigned but five years, she put the clock back a good quarter-century. In terms of absolute progress, Elizabeth took over at about 1530—and so it was that the men of Elizabeth's first years still sported the flat "apprentices'" cap which might have been worn by their grandfathers in 1510.   The effect of Philip's Spanish elegance was not felt until both Philip and Mary had been almost forgotten.

*Round cap, Italian
peasant's, 1565*

Chapter Seven

ELIZABETHAN FASHIONS

NGLAND, in Elizabeth's reign, was the focus of Protes-
tantism, and attempted to spread her doctrines by means
of what we had better call a "cold war." Elizabeth
declared no formal war on any of her European "cousins,"
but sent her troops to harass the Papists at any and every
vulnerable point. Her troops brought back loot with them,
not only in the shape of gold but in the shape of ideas, whether
expressed in phrases or in clothes.

Cunnington has a curious remark in relation to this period:
he says, "Hats and bonnets were worn indoors on all formal
occasions, and at meals up to the 1680s." They were, in fact,
worn at meals by the upper classes until the First World War,
and were worn indoors, in such places as picture-galleries and
City restaurants, until a much later date.

*Woman's hat,
Spanish, 1585*

What I feel that Cunnington means is this: hats were worn
in *one's own house*; a different matter: for they were certainly
worn in the houses of other people until a matter of decades
ago.

It must be stressed that the wearing or not wearing of a hat
or cap is anciently associated with, respectively, subservience
and social freedom. To "cap" a man is not a mediaeval
expression: it is the phrase that a British schoolboy uses to
indicate that he has paid the outward mark of respect to a
superior.

The wearing of a hat, then, is a mark of equality with the
man in whose presence one wears it. And the taking off a
hat in our day is, curiously, not a mark of respect to persons,
but to places. We began (at least, as Christians) with taking
off our hats to the church in which we went: we have ended by
taking off our hats to the automatic lift.

But of "hat-worship," more later. Here we must examine
hat-change, as it occurred in the latter part of the 16th century.

The buttoned cap was still worn far into Elizabeth's reign—and beyond, but it was the mark of the old or the provincial which points the force of Nash's remarking on a "A Sage button cap in the form of a cowshard (cow's turd)." Nash was writing in 1592: the buttoned cap may have been old-fashioned or unfashionable, but had it not been worn, the point would have been lost on Nash's readers.

It is a classic example of Shakespeare's anachronistic fault that he makes his Romans wear "steeple hats," but it should be remembered that the Romans and the Greeks before them wore "steeple" hats; Shakespeare's contemporaries wore them, too. They were called the Capotain hat and were to be, in their regeneration, prolific breeders.

*High-crowned,
English, 1575*

The small "tammy" was also worn; it was the old flat cap without a brim. Yet it was the brimmed hat which was to become the distinguishing mark of Elizabethan elegance. And by "elegance," I mean the wear of the men who mattered: the lesser classes had other tastes, though not less influential than the "toppers" of Sidney and Raleghe and Essex.

Remember, when we are still in Elizabeth's reign, that we are still under the Tudors. Remember, too, their parvenu preoccupation with sumptuary laws. Elizabeth was less honest than her father, and though still seeking to control her subjects' dress, felt no such confidence on the rightness of mere abolition as her father had felt, and invented excuses for her prejudices.

Knitting was imported from the Continent as early as the reign of Edward IV; but, in Elizabeth's reign, the English learnt to knit for themselves. The Government liked knitting not only because knitting used wool but because knitting made wool go a long way, and left the more wool for export.

In the early part of Elizabeth's reign, knitted caps began to be worn, and, in 1570, the immensely powerful Incorporated Company of Hat Makers of London, persuaded the Queen that it would be in the interests of the nation to order her subjects to wear a cap of wool. Accordingly, the Act 13 Eliz. cap. xix laid it down that "euery person . . . shall wear vpon the sabbath and holy day . . . vpon their head a Cap of Wooll knit thicked and dressed in England." The order was made applicable to all persons, except the nobility and "persons of degree," above the age of six years. The knitted caps so ordered to be worn were naturally known as Statute Caps, and were worn by the conscientious and evaded by the fashionable until the Act was repealed in 1597.

Straw hat,
Spanish, 1602

Then there was the stiff "tam-o'-shanter" pleated into a small brim, and a particular point to notice about Elizabethan hats was that no fashionable man, young or old, ever wore a wide brim. Wide-brimmed hats were worn only by parsons, judges, Puritans and by all those others with a financial interest in accusing others of sin. It says much for the Elizabethans that few wore wide brims. Yet, by a common paradox of happening, it was the wide-brimmed Puritan-pragmatical-judgmatical-parsonical hat which was to conquer the small, elegant Elizabethan "topper," and, through Charles as well as Cromwell, to dominate the hundred and fifty years from the Restoration until the beginning of the 19th century.

Historians of costume have differentiated between the "hat" and the "cap" in Elizabethan times; but except for the flat cap with or without brim, there is not more difference among the various tall "hats" and "caps" (or bonnets) of the time than there is between the modern soft hat as worn by two men. A pinch here, a tilt there, and one hat is distinctively Charlie's, the other Les's.

On the subject of Tilting, there is an interesting, odd custom worthy of note. The Court Bonnet, one of the small-crowned Elizabethan caps which carried a jewel and a feather, worn until late in the reign, was always worn on the back of the head at Court functions. Is the phrase, "I tipped my hat" reminiscent of this strange custom?

Our old friend, the Greek *pileus*, acquired the name, Monmouth Cap, in this reign. It was worn by sailors, soldiers and Welshmen: but not more in this reign than in previous reigns. It simply happens that it is noticed in this reign of notable observers, and is given a Welsh, rather than a Greek or Latin name.

Military styles tend, as they did until the end of the following century, to be mere "civilian" styles; but there is evidence that a certain uniformity is being introduced, not so much in the cut of the soldiers' hats, as in the method of wearing them.

Officer's hat,
1581

The carefully executed drawings and paintings of Elizabeth's various processions, notably through London, show the soldiers (marching in threes, as is the modern manner) wearing either flat, soft-topped, small-brimmed bonnets, or fairly wide-brimmed "bowlers" that we shall encounter a century later, in the etching of the coronation procession of James II.

The dress of the Yeomen of the Guard, to which I referred earlier, belongs more properly to the latter part of Elizabeth's reign, than to the early part of her grandfather's; the "Tudor" of the Yeomen's uniform is more Elizabethan than Henrican Tudor.

There is nothing like the sharp eye of the Puritan for recording the nuances of fashion among those whom he hates. Talking of the high-crowned Capotain hats, Stubbes has this to say:

"Sometimes they use them sharpe on the crowne, perking up like a spere or shaft of a steeple, standing a quarter of a yard above the crowne of their heads, some more, some lesse, as please the fantasies of their wavering mindes."

Shakespeare takes us nearer to the contemporary estimation of a Capotain hat than does Stubbes:

O fine villain! a silken doublet! a velvet hose!
a scarlet cloak! and a capotain hat!

English General's
"battle bowler,"
1581

If crowns were high or low, round or flat or "squashed" or "puffed out"; and if brims were wide, small, rolled, non-existent; the Elizabethan hat, like the hat of any other period, had a "cut of the age." The Elizabethans wore what we may certainly call a bowler, and it is not only in the fact that the crown was pleated on, or the fact that the hat-band was a twist of cypress crape, silk and pearls, or silk and spangles that the difference lies between the bowler worn by Sir John Hawkins and that worn by King Edward VII. Shorn of its Elizabethan trimmings, the outline of the late 16th century bowler is very like that of the late 19th century bowler.

We saw how, in the 15th century, hatters were earning themselves a bad name by overcharging. That they were not, in the 16th century, above a little judicious spending of their corporate wealth in bribing the Queen's Highness to enforce their products by Statute, is seen clearly by the Act of 1571.

Prices are instructive, and in noting them, we should observe that the prices quoted follow, not precede, the strengthening of the currency by such economists as Sir Thomas Gresham.

Military musician's hat, 1581

A cap "with a flap in the neck" cost 8*d*. in 1571, ordered by the half-dozen. This was the same price as that quoted in the ordinance of 36 Henry VIII, already mentioned, so that the price had remained stable for nearly thirty years. As money, however, had gained in value through the reformation of the currency, the price had, in terms of real wealth, actually cheapened.

Some prices from 1586 are instructive:

	each
"littell narrow felts lyned with vellett for men"	4*s*. 6*d*.
"braide (broad) Spanish felts"	1*s*. 4*d*.
"graye felts edged and banded"	1*s*. 3*d*.
"cullered felts"	2*s*. 0*d*.
"coullered filt [*sic*] eaten with mothes"	1*s*. 0*d*.

Felt was very popular then, as now; and even as far back as 1430, Lydgate is talking of "fine felt hattes or spectacles to reede," as two of the products most sought after by visitors to London.

We noticed that, in the reign of Edward IV, black (felt) hats were "most genteel"; they remained so into Elizabeth's day, for all that coloured felts were used. One often hears that the association of black with "gentility" is a modern "flight from the warm colours of the past." But the fact is that the preference for black, and the corollary dislike for colours with regard to men's hats, is ancient: the prejudice against coloured civilian headwear was as strong in 1575 as it is today, when "only bookies" are credited with a preference for brown bowlers. It is not without significance that the grey, what is often called "the Ascot," topper, is "correctly" called only the "white" topper: the taboo against colour being present to prevent allusion to the fact that the hat is coloured.

About the beginning of the last quarter of the 16th century, beaver came back into fashion, and remained so until the Restoration; being once more displaced by felt until the end of the 18th century, to remain fashionable again for roughly the same period of time, i.e., until 1860.

The Elizabethan beavers were available in the same colour range obtaining in the early 19th century: brown, black, white, grey—all "sedate" shades. We rarely find that brighter colours were used.

Wide-brimmed, late 16th cent.

Beaver hats were expensive: Stubbes, writing in 1583, says that they could cost "twenty, thirty and forty shillings apiece," and his remark that they were "fetched from beyond the sea whence a great sort of other vanities do come," would appear to indicate France or possibly some other European country as the source. Some readers will remember that the best sort of "beaver," worn before the First World War, were always called "Austrian velours," though they might have come from a place no further than Houndsditch.

In Elizabeth's reign, too, we find another ancient type of hat making its reappearance: the Thrummed hat, that we first encountered in the clothing recovered from the bogs of Jutland. "Thrumming" was weaving in such a manner that the cloth had a nap or pile; and thrummed hats enjoyed a general vogue from the 1560s, until the generality of the vogue confined the wearing of thrummed hats to the less fashionable, the Smart Set adopting Spanish felts as the 16th century drew to a close.

Beside felt and beaver, silk and knitted wool, straw and fur were commonly used for hat-making. Light-weight hats of taffeta, stiffened with buckram, starch or paper, were popular. A hatter's inventory, from the City of Exeter Records, quotes "steerched hatts of Taffeta at 8s. the piece," and mentions "cap paper at 2s. a ream"—obviously a type of "cap paper" inferior to that mentioned in the same inventory: "quyers of strong cap paper, 2s." It is possible that this "cap paper" was not only used for stiffening and lining, but for hat-making on its own account. Many trades used paper hats until a generation ago: the Carpenter in *Alice Through the Looking Glass* wears one.

The brightly coloured linings which were a characteristic of men's hats until a mere generation ago are noted in late Elizabethan times, and possibly had their origin at a much earlier period. It is only in recent years that the social supremacy of one London hatter—or, rather, of his bowler hat—has outmoded all colours but white as lining-colour. But even the "better" hatters of a generation ago were lining their hats with rich crimson satin, a material which had displaced the green of the 18th and 19th centuries on account of the supposed virtue of red in "protecting the head from the dangerous effect of the actinic rays." The pseudo-scientific "reason" for the choice of red indicated clearly enough that the change of colour took place at the latter end of the 19th century.

It is in the trimming of its hats that each generation shows its individuality: even today, though ornamental hat-bands are worn only by Americans and the more demonstratively exhibitionistic of those whose Savile Row is the Charing Cross Road, the hat-band has varied greatly in depth over a mere generation. Indeed, even where a photograph shows a man wearing suit and collar of contemporary cut, the depth of the hat-band will give a certain dating; and today, no less than in the 16th century, the hat-band will indicate both social class and nationality—as well as financial standing.

English countrywoman's high felt, 1585

In Elizabethan times, it gave this information, but conveyed it by less subtle means, though earlier times had been content with plainer hat-bands, as witness the entry, already quoted, in the Durham Almoners Roll: *Pro hatbandys de serico negro, ijs.*

The hat-band, indeed, was a convenient way of indicating real or pretended rank, and was accepted as such. An earlier name for a nobleman at the University—a "tuft" in the 18th and early 19th centuries—was a "gold hat-band"; and

Earle's *Macrocosm* (1628), in the chapter dealing with Your
Gentlemen at the University, has this about a typical under
graduate:

> His companion is ordinarily some stale
> fellow, that ha's beene notorious for
> an ingle to gold hatbands.

There was nothing particularly subtle about old fashion
clothes made the man, and given enough money to cut a dash
any man could, it seems, pass for a gentleman. At a much
later date, Peregrine Pickle needed only to buy himself a good
suit and a gold-laced hat to be "accepted" at once, and the
emphasis on the rank-indicating quality of the hat-band i
Elizabeth's day was strong. But as late as 1849, the report o
Edgar Allan Poe, picked up dying of alcoholic poisoning
stresses that the man, "obviously a gentleman," was wearin
"an old grass hat, with the brim torn, *and with no hat-band.*
(*My italics.*)

Drummer's "pill-box" cap, 1581

The jewels that Benvenuto Cellini mentions as having been
worn in the hat by persons of quality were retained into
Elizabeth's day and beyond, while one curious custom, which
finds echoes in our own day, was the wearing of a lady'
"favour"—her glove or her garter—in the hat-band. The
Earl of Cumberland wore, in his hat, the glove given to him
by the Queen, as can be seen in Nicholas Hilliard's miniature

The hat-band might be made of crewell-work (two thread
worsted) now reserved, by those hatters who sell them to the
green and brown hats of rough, hairy felt, "for sports wear.

Prices are given in the Exeter hatter's inventory quote
above:

"cruell bands"	8*d*. the dozen		
"round silk bands"	6*s*. 0*d*. ,, ,,		
"playen sypars bands"	8*s*. 0*d*. ,, ,,	(i.e., plain cypress)	
"currelled sypars"	12*d*. the yard	(i.e., curled o twisted cypress	
"smooth sypars"	7*d*. ,, ,,		

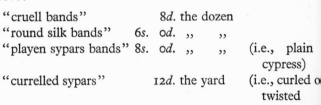

old, silver and copper wire—was extensively used for the
aking of decorative hat-bands and a late 16th century
shion was to wear hat-bands in a "cable twist" of such wire,
ther alone, or mixed with coloured silks. A remark of
ow's points an odd resemblance between English and
hinese rank-indicating custom:

Round-brimmed cap with
feather trimming, man's,
late 16th cent.

As well women as men did wear borders of great cristall
button about their cappes as hat-bands, as a worthy garment to distinguish between the Gentry and others.
(1592)

Nichols's *Progress of Queen Elizabeth* records a gift made
the Queen in 1589: "Hat of tyffany garnished with 28
ttons of golde of one sorte and eight buttons on another
rte about the band and up the feather." (A "button
aze" affected women's fashions, 1908–1910.)
The invaluable Exeter inventory indicates prices of these
ore elaborate bands:

"one golden band wrought upon vellett"	8*s.* each
"one golden band"	6*s.* „
"copper bands"	6*s.* the dozen

The same inventory mentions "bugles" for hat-trimming:
ey were evidently very cheap, which argues some mechanical
mass-productive system of making them: "14 thousand
gells 2*s.* 6*d.*"
By a fortunate chance, many of the jewels worn in Eliza-
ethan hats—the jewel generally served as a clasp to the ostrich
osprey feather—were discovered in 1912, when an old
uilding in Cheapside was being pulled down to make way
r a modern structure.
A workman, digging in the foundations of the old building,
me across a wooden box—crushed, but with its contents
tact. In the box was one of the greatest treasures that the
ity of London has ever yielded up: the stock of an Eliza-
ethan jeweller: brooches, chains, pins, bracelets and other
inkets. The odd thing about this hoard, now unfortunately

scattered among four London museums, instead of being kept intact, is the high proportion, not only of gems much more ancient than the settings, but of gems from a really remote past: there are not only Roman and Greek intaglios and cameos, but even a faience scarab from the Egypt of 1600–1300 B.C. It is true that these very "datable" blue faience scarabs were articles of export to all parts of Europe (one, found under the Hele Stone at Stonehenge, gave the first certain dating of that most famous monument of antiquity), and that the scarab from the Elizabethan jeweller's in Cheapside may well have come from Egypt nearly two thousand years before the Elizabethan shop was opened. Whether or not the gems and ring-bezels were imported, or had been knocking about Britain for two millennia and more, the display found in the shattered box in a Cheapside ruin represents a fair cross-section of what the chic Elizabethan wore in his bonnet, to keep his or her osprey, ostrich and heron's feathers in place.

Prices, as we have seen, were high: when we recall that a firm of popular London hatters were putting out a "Three-and-Ninepenny" in the years before the First World War, we can see how very expensive even a "littell narrow felt lyned with vellet" was, in 1586, at 4s. 6d. Not, indeed, until about 1920, was a beaver (Austrian velour) as dear as £2, so that in terms of relative value the £2 charged for a beaver in Elizabethan times would be the equivalent of some £50 of our money.

Not that the wearers of these expensive hats were unaware of their costliness: there is a line in Florio's *Anglo-Italian Dictionary* of 1598 which indicates that the hats were preciously guarded. Translating *porta beretta*, Florio has: "a capcase, a hat case"—proof, indeed, that the costly felts were treated with some care.

Slashed soldier's bonnet, 1581

The custom of wearing skull- or under-caps continued: the practice extending, not only to the day-time in civil life, but to both day-time and night-time in military life. Those who are interested in the survival power of survivals should remark that the steel undercap, worn under a civilian hat—it was called a "hat piece" or, as Palsgrave (1530) calls it: Cappe of fence:

segrette de maille—survived long after the cloth or silk under-cap had gone out of use: certain regiments of the British Army using it until well into the 19th century.

Coifs, as has been noted before, were worn by old men and lawyers[1]: the former liked black coifs, the latter white. The prices for 1571 are "velvet coif, 2*s*. 6*d*.; silk coif, 2*s*."; but a Machyn reference to a cap embroidered with pearls and precious stones implies that there were caps more elaborate, and costlier, than those marketed at 2*s*. and 2*s*. 6*d*.

Embroidered night cap, early 17th cent.

The Night Cap was, as in previous times, a cap for the evening, rather than a cap in which one slept. There are some fine examples in the Victoria and Albert Museum, of white silk, quilted with a delicate embroidery in coloured silks. The crown is high and rounded; the brim, cut in four pointed half-ovals, is turned up close to the crown. This pattern survived until the 18th century, and its persistence in fashion may be attributed to the fact that the women of the family making these caps as a labour of familial duty, if not of familial love, the pattern was inherited from generation to generation.

There was, again as in previous times, the "night cap" as we call it: that is, to be worn in bed. It could be made of any material, to suit the fancy and the pocket of the wearer, but generally it was of wool or linen, usually white. It often had strings, for tying under the chin. It was called the Biggin—a word which, as we have already noted, is still used (only slightly altered) to describe the leather hat of the Billingsgate fish-porters.

Hats for women were the innovation of fashion in Elizabeth's reign. At the beginning of the reign, the headwear which had been popular in the previous three reigns still continued both in common and in fashionable use: the French and "Mary Stuart" hoods survived the coming of Elizabeth—the former until the end of the 16th century, the latter until the beginning of Charles I's reign. Made generally of lawn or linen, and often trimmed with lace (except when, black, it was worn as

[1] Serjeants-at-Law wore the coif until the very end of their Order in the 19th century.

mourning, or by widows), the hood, French or "Mary Stuart
naturally showed some changes with the years. But the ma
distinguishing marks of each type of hood was preserved un
each went out of fashion: the French hood with straight lir
over the forehead, the "Mary Stuart" with the line over tl
forehead wired to dip in a broad "U."

The Bongrace and the Cornet remained until the ne
century: the flattening of the forehead line in the French hoc
turning it, as we have said, into the Bongrace, which, whe
elaborated with lace, was known as the Shadow. But tl
Shadow does not appear until about 1580, when it supplante
the velvet Bongrace in popular favour.

Bongrace, 1550

These women's head-dresses were quite costly, the price
a cornet, in 1559, being given as 4s. 8d., a "bonnegrace" as 4
The Billiment and the Paste were still used; but it is, of cours
for the reintroduction of the cap, bonnet or hat for women th
this reign is chiefly memorable in the history of fashion. Tl
important point to note about this reintroduction of tl
woman's hat, is that the first models were merely "feminized
men's hats, and it was not until the beginning of the 19
century that a distinctive style of hat for women was evolve

It is one of the more curious inexplicabilities in huma
record that, our chronology being "quite arbitrary," tl
divisions of each century show an odd likeness from centui
to century. The Elizabethan woman adopted man's hats ;
the end of the 16th century; the Restoration woman took 1
wearing man's hats at the end of the 17th century; and at tl
end of the 18th century, and at the end of the 19th centur;
the same thing happened: the hats worn by women at the en
of the 19th century seem the most masculine of all only becaus
the real masculine prototype was plain.

Only because the masculine hat of the latter part of the 16t
century was itself an ornate, "effeminate," affair do tl
"masculine" hats of the Elizabethan women seem to have
marked "femininity." In fact, they were just as masculir
as the Homburgs, trimmed with half-a-grouse, that our twee
clad aunts and great-aunts wore in the years around 1895.

Women always adopt men's fashions in periods of grea

cial change: and if the end of Elizabeth's reign seems, to
storians, nothing like as fundamentally disturbed, socially
eaking, as were the ends of the 17th, 18th and 19th centuries,
ey should look again at what was happening to a world which
oduced *Love's Labour's Lost*, the stocking-frame and the
st tentative English grasp at the vast Empires of the East and
the West.

Perhaps the favourite man's style in women's hats was the
all bonnet, with pleated, tam o' shanter crown, and small
owlerish" brim. The popular name for this pretty little
t, which, the first real hat to be adopted by women, lasted
e thirty years from 1565 to 1595, was the "Taffeta Pipkin."

male origin was always apparent in the tilt with which
men wore it. The Court Bonnet, which differed from the
ffeta Pipkin only in that the former had no brim, properly
eaking, was also adopted by the women: both being worn
rched on top of hair contained within hair-net, plain under-
p or jewelled caul.

Taffeta pipkin, 1585

The caps which had begun to be worn by women in the very
rly part of the century, continued to be worn into Elizabeth's
gn. The first to vanish was the small, brimless "beret,"
rn over an undercap, whose sides projected to cover the ears
form "cheek-pieces." This had gone by 1560. The
ttice cap lasted a further twenty years, but is rarely seen
er 1580.

After the caps, the Court bonnet, beginning its run in about
75, continued in favour for the next ten years, during which
e Court bonnet's successors gradually developed.

From the pill-box-like Court bonnet, women inevitably
ogressed to the Elizabethan versions of the Bowler and the
pper—this with a tall crown widening as it went upwards,
a manner reminiscent of the beavers of 1810 as well as the
potain hat. Like the hats of the men, all these women's
ts bore the feather secured with a jewelled clasp, which is a
aracteristic of Elizabethan headwear, and the materials used
re usually as rich as those used by men. On the other hand,
e evidence of contemporary portraits—see that of Lady
illoughby, in the National Portrait Gallery—shows that,

like the Victorian woman of, say, the 1860s, the Elizabethan women could wear a hat of exceptional, almost, one might say, of excessive, plainness.   A further Elizabethan characteristic fashion associated with hats was the habit of tilting the hat forward.   This is a recurrent phenomenon, and has recently been adopted by the neo-Edwardians as the "correct" mode of wearing their hats—"soft" or "hard."

That the wearing of tall hats had spread to the more prosperous of the middle class was noted by Platter, the German traveller, though the low-crowned Bowler or Wide-awake was occasionally to be seen.

Exceptions to all these fashion-rules must be made for the City of London, whose obstinate rejection of the Mode had political, social and religious bases.   The term "Cap of Wool" came to mean a tradesman or a citizen (the same thing in those days), and it took more than Dekker's sneers to laugh the City man's wife into spending the money of which she was so proud, on following the mode.   Even after the Restoration, when much of the calculated "separateness" of the City had been broken down, pretty Mrs Pepys was still an exception.   Anyway, she was French, and though Pepys lived in the City, he was a Court man.

Woman's, late 16th cent.

A line in Eden's *Treatise of the New Indies*, published in the first year of Mary Tudor's reign, may give a clue to the change from the low, soft hat to the high, stiff hat: a change which began in Spain, spread to France, and so to England.   It is true that the Elizabethan "topper" may have its origins in the tall Burgundian cap of the late 15th century; for this hat was worn in the Spanish Netherlands, and was certainly worn by the Spanish and Portuguese admirals.   Nevertheless, I feel that, in this tall-hat fashion, we have one of the first examples of the influence that the New World was destined to exercise over the Old.

Eden, talking of the "Indians," says: "Some weare high cappes, lyke myters, of redde colour."   One may imagine that these hats were brought back to Spain as curiosities, and that they inspired the Spanish tall-hat fashion which was to spread over Europe before the turn of the 16th century.

Cauls not only remained "in," but were destined to acquire a fashionable prominence in the early part of the succeeding century which caused them, when brought back to notice by the Romantic painters and novelists of post-Napoleonic days, to be reintroduced in the self-conscious "Charles I" fashions of the 1830s.

Cauls, of network which might or might not be jewelled, but which was generally bright with tinsel, were often lined, and this lining could have a social significance, in that it might be indicative of the wearer's rank.

The Coif, which is really the Caul made from whole cloth, instead of from netted threads, continued. In Elizabethan times, there was a Caul made with a slight point over the forehead, the sides being cut away at the temples, but covering ears and cheeks. It was tied under the chin, and was popularly known as "cheeks and ears." Like the Caul, the Coif could be plain—it was so when worn in bed, whether or not one was ill—or it could be embroidered as richly as the taste and purse of the wearer counselled.

Widow wearing chaperon hood and barbette, early 16th cent.

Another article of head-wear was the Forehead Cloth: a triangular piece of material, one straight edge of which was bound around the forehead, the sides being pinned at the back of the head or under the chin, a point being left to hang down the back of the head.

The New Year's gifts to Queen Elizabeth in 1564 included "A cawle and three forehead cloths of cammeryk netted with gold."

"The use of *Forehead Cloths*," says Cunnington, "is uncertain. They might have been worn to prevent wrinkles. They were definitely worn during illness." And Cunnington then quotes Fynes Moryson, writing in 1617: "Many weare such crosse-clothes or forehead cloathes as our women use when they are sicke."

The reason for the forehead or cross cloth seems plain to see: they were merely "detachable linings" for the caul, enabling the caul to be worn without its spangles and bugles and jewels catching in the hair.

Nevertheless, the assumed connection of the forehead cloth

8—H.H.

with illness has been maintained in a curious manner: today, the only women who still use the forehead cloth are the members of the Nursing profession. Nuns of certain Orders also use it, but here the continuity is more conscious; and the forehead cloth has been retained by tradition strengthened with a religious sanction.

Traditions of what we may call the "trivial" kind are not only extraordinarily tenacious on human behaviour, but go back often further than we think. Thus, when Van Meteren, in 1575, in discussing the hat-habits of the English women, says, "Married women only wear a hat both in the street and in the house; those unmarried go without a hat . . ." he mentions a custom which persists, at least among our older ladies, to this day: that of wearing a hat indoors, especially when entertaining guests to luncheon.

The no-hat fashion, about which both the professional carpers and the professional hatters complain, is no new thing; no novel "lapse into slipshod ways." As the passage shows, the custom of walking out bareheaded was practised by young women at least as long ago as 1575.

Then, of course, there are those caps and hats, both for men and for women, which fall into no definable class; hats which are so "basic" that one meets them on a Greek vase, or in a Winchester manuscript or on an Elizabethan tapestry. These are the immortals among hats. One sees them, and yet never sees them in shops. But they are here, in Elizabeth I's reign, just as they were in all previous times, and have been since. There is a tapestry cushion cover in the Victoria and Albert Museum on which skilful fingers have depicted a mounted man, hawking: he wears such a hat. Hats possessed by both Mr Neville Chamberlain and Mr Harold Macmillan might well have come from the same, ancient, mysterious and everlasting source.

That fruitful source of hat-fancy, the Army, was not properly into its stride as the 16th century came to an end, but there are indications that uniformity of colour and cut in the man's clothing was already an ideal after which Authority was seeking; even though an order of 1594 laid down that coats were "to be of such colours as you can best provide." Never-theless, the idea—as well as the ideal—of "uniform" is present in most writings which deal with the servants, armed or otherwise, of the Crown.

Later we shall consider the development of the postman's uniform, but here an early reference to getting "the post" into uniform may be noted.

In 1590, the Council of Aberdeen ordered, for Alexander Taylor, "the post," a livery of blue cloth, with the armorial bearings of the town worked in silver on his right sleeve.

There is no mention of Sandy Taylor's hat; but there is a mention of the headwear worn by the archers of the levy raised in Lancashire in 1577: "skulls of iron, worn under a Scotch bonnet."

The engraving of *The Funerall Roll of Sir Philip Sidney*, to which reference has already been made, provides us with a better idea of what had been happening to military dress than any written record of the time.

These soldiers, so clearly depicted in the engraving, are not yet in what we have come to think of a "uniform," but that their dress is uniform there can be no doubt.

"Bowler," 1580

But to return to these soldiers of 1587, who march with arms reversed, followed by a man in a black hood with ground-length liripipe. "The puffed and bombastic lower wear," says W. Y. Carman, in his *British Military Uniforms*, "is not for these men, and they all wear knee-length breeches. The long netherstocks are replaced by stockings, either below or above the breeches. The padded peascod doublet is out of fashion, and the short loose coat is worn. The head-dress is the most striking change: gone is the flat cap. Even the poked-up bonnet is not shown, and a hat with a high, domed crown, something like an elongated bowler, is worn; officers have one side of the brim turned up and held in place by a jewel; around the base of the hat is a narrow twisted turban; scarves of cypress with fringed ends are worn in the hat bands."

In a further reference to the military head-dress in late Elizabethan times, the same authority says: "It has been mentioned that the hat and hat-cap were replacing the bonnet.

The hat-cap was probably made of pieces of cloth sewn together like a brimmed hat, and coming to a point at the top. The true hat made with a wide brim and a flat top was more an article of the end of the century." It was, once introduced, to remain an article of British naval and military uniform until the present day.

Chapter Eight

"CAVALIER" HATS OF THE 17TH CENTURY

IN 1603 Queen Elizabeth the First, the Last Tudor, died, to be succeeded by the son of the woman Elizabeth had put to death.

Wide-brimmed, 1640

The history of James's reign, as of James's character, abounds in apparent contradictions; but here we are concerned more with the contradictions of dress than with those of royal emotions or national politics.

We have only rarely noticed the accessories of dress which went with the various hats and caps that we have discussed: but there was, and is, a close tie between the hat and the style of hair-dressing; between the style of hair-dressing and the treatment of neck and shoulders.

The small Elizabethan hats—"little apish hats from France" —were the only possible type to be worn with the ruffs and rebates—wired collars—which, beginning in no modest dimension in about 1550, grew in size and complication as the century progressed. Possibly of all fashions of past times, the vast ruffs and rebates of the period, 1580–1620, are the best known: the reason being that it was in the ruff-wearing period that a revival of Northern European art took place, and the artists, French, Dutch and English, have left a generous record of ruff-wearers.

The wide-brimmed hat does not go with the ruff or with the wired stand-up collar called a rebate: yet, with the coming of James, this incongruity was introduced, and what is more, persisted for a generation, until rather than give up the wide-brimmed hat, men and women substituted the fall-down collar for the upstanding one.

The ruff might have prevented the wide-brimmed hat from bring reintroduced: for a time both ruff and large hat competed for existence on the same person. In the end, it was the hat, and not the ruff, which won.

Broad-brimmed, 1642

The tall, wide-brimmed hat is always associated with James I, and it is curious, to say the least, that the hat popularly accepted as the headgear peculiar to "witches" should be regarded as so peculiarly the headgear of the learned author of a violent denunciation of witches and witchcraft: James I.

James wore both the tall-crowned, wide-brimmed hat, and the cartwheel ruff, which must have touched the brim of the hat every time that the wearer bent his head only a little backwards.

After the change in headwear had driven the upstanding ruffs away, so that the "falling band," encountered as early as 1540, took its place, the professions continued to use it for many years—to this day, the cartwheel ruff ("He looks in that deep ruff like a head in a platter," says Ben Jonson, in *The Alchemist*) is worn by clergymen of the Lutheran Church in Scandinavia. They also wear a top-hat, so much more sensible with a cartwheel ruff than a wide-brimmed hat.

The point to bear in mind about the hat fashions for the whole of Europe in the early 17th century is that, whether or not the crown of the hat was tall or shallow, the brim was large. This brim was to vary in width from generation to generation, but not until the end of the 18th century was the brim of any fashionable hat to revert to the small dimensions that it had attained in Elizabeth's time.

When we come to consider the hats of the 18th century, we shall notice that the prevailing characteristic, throughout the century, is the "cock" in all its varieties; that is, the turning up, pinching and at times shaping of the brim, to produce the characteristic 18th century "three-cornered" shape.

But the "cock" is a great deal more ancient than the 18th century: it was that century's genius to regulate and formalize the "cock"—that is all. Again and again the "cock" appears in the history of the hat, mostly for the reason that, short of stiffening the brim of a wide-brimmed hat until the felt is as stiff as wood, a "cock" is inevitable, to counteract the inevitable droop of the brim.

We have seen how the officers marching in Philip Sidney's funeral procession wore fairly wide-brimmed, high-crowned hats, with the brim turned up, the men wearing the brim not so "cocked." Now, with the dawn of the 17th century, the wide-brimmed hat is back again and so, inevitably, is the "cock."

Here are fashions which are as familiar to the ordinary person of today as they were to the wearers: the art of such painters as Rubens and Rembrandt, Van Dyck and Frans Hals —particularly of Hals—has made the clothes and the wearers extraordinarily familiar to us all. One painting alone, that of the reproduced-in-its-thousands *Laughing Cavalier* of Frans Hals, has made the more "romantic" type of 17th century wide-brimmed black hat as famous as any hat could ever be. But all the Dutch painters of that time, masters and mediocrities, have recorded on canvas and wood and paper the two characteristic appearances of the early 17th century: the tall-crowned, wide-brimmed hat over the cartwheel ruff, and the tall-crowned, wide-brimmed hat over the "falling band" or "falling ruff" and practically, there was not much difference between them.

Wide-brimmed, 1635

One curious aspect of the reintroduction of the "falling band" was the "repeat motif" which was apparent in the boots. The boot-tops fell down to below the knee, even to mid-calf, and were filled up with lace to match that of the falling ruff. It must be confessed that some of the men of the time, as seen in the contemporary portraits, present an appearance ludicrous enough: tall, conical, wide-brimmed hats, falling ruffs which give them "hock bottle" shoulders, short cloaks, shorter, beltless doublets, shirts tumbling out of their waistbands and boots which hang about the ankles. It was no wonder, with fashions like that dominant, that the clergy, the law, medicine and other professions clung desperately to the sartorial relics of the past: to the hooded gowns and hanging sleeves and trencher caps worn over velvet undercaps—the "mortar board" that both the Americans and we retain academically to this day.

After 1620, the brim of the hat became even broader than it had been in the first years of the century: its crown was not tall, but the wide brim, turned up, conceals the crown altogether in pictures, as doubtless it must have done in actual wear.   The other type of wide-brimmed hat, associated for ever with the dour man-haters gloomily regarding the cavalier's little boy in that pictorial classic of the nursery, *When Did You Last See Your Father?*, was the 17th century version of the preceding century's Capotain or Copintank hat.   This is the famous Sugar Loaf hat of the Parliamentarians and general burgess class; and in the years from 1620 to the end of James II's reign, it was to have a political, religious and business significance—being pre-eminently the hat of Nonconformism, Republicanism and that curiously soulless money-grubbing which, in the 19th century, regulated itself into a system, and called itself "Liberalism."

Wide-brimmed, 1635

As the century progressed, this pre-eminently odd-man-out hat got lower in the crown, tending to become slightly smaller in the brim—the brim becoming flatter; and the whole hat taking on that precise look that we associate with the modern bowler or the Homburg in the hatter's window.   This flattish hat—the "wide awake" that we shall meet again in the 19th century—was not confined in use to the Republicans: not only did the soldiers of James II's reign wear it, but that prim voluptuary, James himself, as well as his apoplectic dog, Baron Jeffreys of Wem, wore it.   But it was still the hat of the Quakers' choice.

The 18th century was a very hat-conscious century: but so, too, was the 17th.   Yet there is a difference: the 18th century's hat-consciousness was based on social rank—never so much in men's minds as when some social revolution is permitting hordes of climbers to overstep the rigid divisions of caste.   In the 17th century, the hat-consciousness peculiar to that age of revolution was based, as may well be understood, not so much on the consciousness of rank as on the consciousness of politico-religious affiliations.

High-crowned, man's or woman's, 1650

Hats and caps were always worn indoors—a custom which was to be maintained by the upper classes until well into this present century: being abandoned only under the pressure exerted from socially inferior classes.

Rationalization of customs has always been a human failing;

and the 17th century could find "reasons" for its indoors hat-wearing: "Got a strange cold in me head," Pepys records, "by flinging off my hat at dinner." The writer recalls that, when he visited City restaurants—"chop-houses"—as a boy, he was fascinated by the rising and falling motion of the silk-hats on the earnest lunchers' heads, as the jaws worked steadily away at the "chop and two veg."

Wide-brimmed, tall crowned, 1665

The history of the hat must take account of its rise in social esteem—and occasional fall—as evidenced by the "rationing" of its use. In the 17th century, it was worn everywhere: or, rather, it is more correct to say that men hardly ever went uncovered.

According to Pepys, they even wore a hat in church, as Jews do to this day—"A simple fellow . . . exclaiming against men's wearing their hats in the church." But this remark needs some analysis: it was the custom, up to the destruction of Old St Paul's by fire, to treat the ancient cathedral as a vast piazza, in which hawkers, stall-holders, whores and mere idlers were always to be found: the centre of this promenade being the tomb of Duke Humphrey of Gloucester—whence the expression, "to dine with Duke Humphrey": that is, to take a walk in St Paul's instead of eating, because one lacked the money for a dinner.

One, then, could look on a church as a place in which to loiter—when one wore one's hat—or a place in which to worship: in which case one did not.

The Puritans were exceedingly hat-conscious: their attitude towards head-coverings being fanatically ritualistic and sacramental.

Puritan writings of this period are full of defences of this custom of staying covered in the presence of one's fellows; and full of denunciations of what the Puritans called "hat worship," "cap worship" or "hat honour." We have already quoted Bishop Hall: "We hold the head uncovered if the hat be off, though the cap be on"; but this did not suit the Puritans.

In 1669, William Penn, the eponymous founder of Pennsylvania, thought it worth his time to write a book on the subject:

No Cross, No Crown: or Several Solid Reasons against Hat-Honour, Titular Respects, You to a Single Person.

And, in 1677, we find George Fox asking solemnly in his *Journal*, "if this hat-honour and showing the bare head be an invention of man and not from God?"

As an invention of man, it is ancient enough. Mandeville, writing *circa* 1400, says, "He doffez his hatte," and, *circa* 1430, we find in Freemasonry: "When thou comest by-fore a lorde . . . hod (*hood*) or cappe that thou of do."

And, in Lord Berners's translation of Froissart (1523), we find:

Tall-crowned, 1665

"He toke of his cap and saluted the duke."

From kings and dukes, lesser persons got the courtesy, and in spite of William Penn's remark that "Honour was from the Beginning, but Hat respect and most Titles, were of late," one may well understand that, by 1659, Cleveland is writing: "He is punctual in exacting your hat."

For women, as the century turned, the hat, as we have seen, followed the change in masculine fashion: the small bonnets and "top hats" gave way to the large-brimmed, high-crowned hat, often adorned with a feather. This hat remained in fashion among women until almost the end of the century; but whereas, in the early part of the 17th century, the hat was worn over an embroidered undercap, the undercap did not survive the Restoration. "Mary Stuart" hoods were still worn, and various head-coverings were carried over from the last century, save, as we have said, the small bonnets. Widows wore long veils, lappets and other marks of their state—"widows' weeds"—and these were to be worn, at least in the more traditional parts of America, until beyond the first half of the 19th century. Mrs Clemm, Edgar Allan Poe's aunt, was wearing a full set of black and white head-coverings proper to widows, in 1850; and within my own recollection is the sight of a widow whom I knew when I was about twenty. She wore a goffered framing to her face, and a veil of black crape. Possibly some very conservative old ladies are wearing such headgear to this day.

Woman's hat, 1617

It must be borne in mind that the "Cavalier" hats worn by women in the days between 1600 and the Restoration were worn only out-of-doors: indoors, the charming "caul" fashion returned, though the caul was smaller, and sometimes was little more than a "skull cap." The hair was released from the confinement of a net, and dressed in a free, natural fashion, as may be seen in any of the many portraits of women surviving from that time.

It was inevitable that women's fashions, during the Commonwealth, should have been marked by a lack of ostentation; but, unlike those of the men, they were marked by extraordinary good taste as well. For the first time we see coats and skirts cut on modern lines: sometimes with so advanced an appearance that, when we meet them again in Victorian times, we see that no change has taken place. The early Victorian neck-line, with the edge of the bodice stretching from shoulder to shoulder exposing a good deal of bust, was seen during the latter part of the Commonwealth; but the "players-safe" covered this expanse of naked neck and chest with a plain linen or muslin collar which closed tightly up the throat and fell over the shoulders almost to mid upper-arm. The hats were of the plain, masculine type: like late 18th century toppers with rather larger brims, and the more fashionable women adorned them with plumes of ostrich.

The small linen caps were worn indoors, and sometimes out; and a charming fashion was the loose hoods of wool cloth or velvet, which tied under the chin. It is often stated that these were worn only by the middle or lower classes, but there is no evidence that this was so. There is, for instance, a famous portrait of Madame de Maintenon, wearing one of these hoods. They survived among the more conservative elements until the end of the 18th century.

With the Restoration, luxury came back, or in our modern phrase, "austerity" went out. Yet, for all the "austerity" of the first half of the century, prices were high, and new materials were constantly being introduced by the hatters.

There might have been unrest at home, but it was unrest based on fundamental social changes, and those changes were

Lace-trimmed fillet, 1625

High-crowned, feather-trimmed, 1660

based on a vast access of wealth. At last, England had suc-
cessfully planted colonies, and the colonies needed goods.
Behind most of the religion and republicanism was the ferment of new-found opportunities of wealth.

"Shag," a material that we shall encounter again in the 19th
century, was popular; and according to Beck, *Draper's Dictionary*, is a rough, hairy material, "generally made of worsted,
but at times wholly of hair or silk." It has now acquired the
"nicer" name of "hatter's plush."

Cunnington quotes from the accounts of Ben Frewen,
haberdasher, preserved in the archives of the Sussex Archaeological Collection: "for a fine straw hat, lined in the brims
£1 4s. 0d." (1632); and a beaver hat was even more expensive,
a good hat of this material costing between £3 and £4. Even
in 1616, we find, "Your four-shillings Dutch felt shall be
converted to a three-pound beaver."

The beaver hat was called a Castor; an inferior type of
"beaver," made partly of beaver and partly of coney, was
termed a demi-castor.

An account of 1648 gives: "For a French castor and a band
£1 12s. 6d.—a relatively cheap one; but "a demi-castor hat,"
stolen in 1645, was valued at only one shilling."

All hats were lined; hat-bands were of ribbon, silk, crewel-
work, plain cloth, a row of buttons, and cable twist of metal,
either gold, silver or copper. Bunches of ribbons came in
about 1640 and survived the Restoration. Feathers, as we
have seen, were worn in the hat, and these continued to be
worn until the end of the 18th century by civilians; by senior
officers in various armies, and by royal and imperial coachmen
and footmen, they are worn to this day.

Caps, except for the old, the unfashionable and the rustic,
were "out"; but here again tradition as distinct from fashion
had a say. Knights of the Garter and royal pages not only
wore ceremonially the old-fashioned trunk-hose and doublet,
but the flat-cap, adorned with heron's feathers. Garter
knights still do, but the dress of the pages has been "modern-
ized" to an 18th century type.

Feather-trimmed, 1665

The Yeomen of the Guard, and certain professions also

stuck to the cap. Soldiers continued to wear the Monmouth
cap: a tall, sugar-loaf, brimless affair. The flat cap was also
the correct wear for liveried servants, and so continued in use
until the powdered wig displaced the flat cap as the headwear
of the flunkey.

It was in the 17th century that the wig, long used as substitute for natural hair, either for those who had lost it all or
those who needed more than Nature had left to them, entered
upon its long career as a fashion in itself: beginning at some
time after the Restoration, and continuing in ordinary civilian
use, until the beginning of the 19th century.

Periwig, late 17th cent.

The Church—in the person of the Archbishop of Canterbury—discontinued the use of the wig in 1862; but the
justiciaries of all those nations whose law is based upon that of
England wear the wig, save only the United States of America.

No more extraordinary fashion has had a couple of contin-
ents in its grip than this fashion of wearing an unnecessary wig;
and no extraordinary fashion has maintained its grip on all
classes and all professions for so long. At the end of the
period over which the fashion continued, even the common
soldier had to be put into a wig as part of his "issue" uniform.

It is commonly asserted that the wig, at first long and curly,
hanging down over the shoulders like the hyacinthine ears of a
spaniel, was adopted in flattery of the young King Louis XIV,
whose luxuriant chestnut hair was one of his principal physical
attractions. This may be, but what is certain is that the
fashion was brought over from France into England.

Charles II's sister, Minette, had married the brave but
exceedingly effeminate Monsieur, brother to the King, and a
person whom we should expect to see wearing any extravagance that fashion permitted. In fact, the pictures of Monsieur show him in a wig looking like a black bee-skep, while he
is tricked out with short "bolero" jacket, lace-trimmed
"shorts" and enough ribbon to tie-up chocolate boxes for a
life-time.

Monsieur, though his dress shows obvious exaggerations,
was not the only one to wear it. One needed to be hearty
indeed not to look an effeminate freak in this absurd style; but

Pleated night-cap, 1690

Wide-brimmed, 1670

by the last quarter of the century the doublet and jerkin had given way to the frock and the waistcoat, a style which, with modifications, is still with us. The hat, from being flat-brimmed, with a flat-topped, tall crown, became low-crowned, with a fairly narrow brim, slightly curled (the "Quaker" hat mentioned earlier), and where feathers were worn, they were worn within the circumference of the brim.

Before we leave the 17th century, let us look at what was worn on their heads by the women. This part of our history is not notable for any great variety of style; rather were the old fashions discontinued than that many new were introduced. The large Cavalier hat continued in fashion after the Restoration; among the less fashionable, the old custom of wearing the large hat over a coif was still observed—as late as the very end of the 17th century. But for the elegant the fashion was to go out of doors bareheaded, or with very little on the head. The Cornet, a sort of coif fitting the back of the head, with lappets which hung down over the shoulders remained in use, if not altogether in fashion, but the really distinctive headgear of the period 1690 to 1710 was the Fontange, a many-tiered "top-knot" of starched linen and lace, kept erect on a wire frame called the Commode.

The Fontange resembled, in shape, a half-opened fan, and was arranged to spring upright from just above the forehead. It was attached to a close-fitting linen cap, worn, like the Cornet, at the back of the head; but sometimes, as may be seen from contemporary pictures, it was attached to a close fitting, face-encircling, hood, with strings tying under the chin. Often the facial opening of the hood was edged with lace.

At the back of the cap or hood, two long linen or lace streamers were attached, and these either hung down, or were pinned up to the crown. The hair itself was wired up on a frame or "Palisade," and was arranged to "sit" before the Fontange.

Artificial curls were attached when necessary, and when many of these were needed to build up the Fontange, they were collectively known as a Tour or Tower.

Woman wearing font-ange, 1695

Chapter Nine

MILITARY UNIFORMS AND THE
GREAT REBELLION

O<small>NE</small> accident gave the hat a great and unusual importance in the first half of the 17th century. When the
Great Rebellion broke out, the combatants in that
civil war were not only of the same race, but generally of the
same interests. What is more, men would change sides not
only before or after battles but even during them: sometimes
with unfortunate results to themselves.

When Sir Faithful Fortescue brought his troop over to
King Charles's side at the battle of Edgehill, seventeen or
eighteen of the repentant rebels lost their lives: they had not
removed their orange scarves quickly enough to be recognized
by the Royal troops as recruits. Sashes were the distinguishing mark of the soldiery at this period when the "uniform,"
in our modern sense of the word, had yet to be introduced.
But sashes had certain disadvantages: the principal being that,
unless they were of one, or at the most, two colours, they were
not easily recognized, while, if of no more than two colours,
they were quite likely to be found on both sides.

It became evident that clear, instant recognition was something which had to be devised and "recognition signals"
tended to be placed in the hat. Though scarves continued
for many decades to be *the* distinguishing mark of allegiance
in general, and attachment to a certain corps in particular, the
use of the hat to carry the necessary identification is found at
the very beginning of the Great Rebellion. Writing home to
the Doge and Senate of the Most Serene Republic, the
Venetian Ambassador to the Court of St James reported that
the Royalists were distinguished from the rebels by wearing
"rose-coloured bands on their hats"—another example of the
significance attaching to a hat-band.

Where armour was worn—and it was Cromwell's

"anachronistic" reintroduction of full plate-armour for his "Ironsides" which was the "secret weapon" determining the outcome of *that* war—the helmets were of two types: the comb-helmet (morion) worn by the pikemen, and still seen in the ceremonial garb of the halberdiers of the Honourable Artillery Company, and the "lobster," worn by cavalrymen.

This morion, historically associated with "stout Cortes" and the rest of the Conquistadores, had changed somewhat in the century and more which had elapsed since the conquest of Mexico and Peru. The "lunette" curve of the side-view had been flattened out, until, in Cromwell's day, the helmet had assumed a form not unlike that of the steel helmets worn by the French troops in the First World War. The protective "comb" on the helmet was always (if we may believe such careful drawings as those of Joseph de Gheyn) worn with a plume of feathers, and the difference in colouring of these plumes made for a simple military recognition system. It is curious that an even simpler system, invented three hundred years later, with the reintroduction of the steel casque, was not adopted: that of stencilling the mark. But feather badges served, though there was always the additional mark of the coloured scarf.

The other type of helmet familiar from pictures of the Civil War battles was the so-called "lobster" helmet, named thus from its articulated steel "curtain" which gave protection to the back of the neck. This had a wrought-iron visor, which, while offering no protection against the pinking of a rapier, would withstand the cut of a cavalry broadsword.

It is of interest here to note that the late Middle Ages lingered on in this war: some of the combatants wearing full armour, with closed helmets. At Hopton Heath, in 1643, the Earl of Northampton was so completely encased in steel that, when his enemies unhorsed him, they had to remove his helmet to administer the *coup de grâce*.

Not all troops wore steel or iron helmets. The musketeers wore broad-brimmed hats made either of felt or of leather: these usually carried a hat-band of some distinctive colour, to enable the wearer to be "recognized."

Indeed, as the Civil War progressed, it is easy to see that the hat came more and more to be regarded as the most suitable vehicle for carrying the necessary recognition marks.

It is possibly the mistrust that each side had of the loyalty of the men fighting under its command which prevented the establishment of permanent recognition-marks. Pass-words were issued at the latest possible moment—usually just before giving battle—"The enemie's word was 'Queen Mary,' ours, 'God is our Strength'—and so he was indeed"; and the last-minute selection and issue of agreed recognition marks, to be worn in the hats, were more in the nature of "visible pass words" than regimental and corps badges in our understanding of the phrase.

This explains why it was that, at Marston Moor, the Republicans wore a piece of white paper or a white handkerchief in their hats. When, at this same battle, the cavalry under Fairfax was defeated, all that Fairfax had to do was to take the white handkerchief from his hat, and pass, unmolested, through the Royalist lines to safety. Obviously, something more certain than this temporary device had to be adopted, to tell friend from foe. "They had beane stalks in their hats, we nothing; some of ours of their owne accord had white Linnen, or paper in their hats." At the battle of Newbury, Essex's men fastened green boughs in their hats; an idea, Carman suggests, brought over from the Continent: the habit, he adds, persisted until well on into the following century.

The Civil War—it was fought out in Holland as well as in England, Scotland, Wales and Ireland—emphasized the essential quality of recognition or "field" marks, especially when needing to distinguish between troops of the same nation. This need made for the stressing of the hat's importance in a new aspect: as a bearer of the necessary recognition marks.

But it is interesting to note that social improvement was held to be related to, and marked by, a change of hat. Part of the civilizing mission of the Anglo-Scots rulers of that time was—according to a letter written to the Earl of Sutherland by his uncle, Sir Robert Gordon—to "take away the reliques of Irish barbarity which as yet remain in your country, to wit the

9—H.H.

Irish (i.e., Gaelic) language and the habit; purge your country piece by piece from that uncivil kind of clothes, such as plaids, mantles, trues *and blew bonnets*[1]; make severe acts against those that shall wear them." A Scots chieftain, MacNaughton, writes, at the same period, that his men "cannot muster before your lordship in their plaids *and blue caps*."[1] Scottish sentimentality, in respect of Scotia's ancient dress dates, only from, and is in fact the creation of, two sentimentally romantic Germans: Queen Victoria and the Prince Consort.

Though Cromwell polished off the Levellers and Fifth Monarchy men, and the other communistical minorities within the larger movement of Republicanism, non-conformist die-hards imposed their fashions on the Restoration: especially in the matter of hats—or, rather, *the* hat. Their dress, too: plain jerkin, small boy's "knickers," with straight, up-and-down legs, "sensible" shoes and plain, wide, "falling band" (or collar). This might not have been the dress of the fashionable few, but it was the dress of the prosperous many; and even the ribbon-fluttering dress of the exquisite was basically the plain dress of the Puritan, with foolish adornments added.

Low-crowned
"bowler," 1685

The "ideal of the English gentlemen: dark, sober clothes, of plain cut"—as one so often hears it expressed—is the heritage of those times. It took many years for the bleak Puritan ideal to triumph; to offer itself in the guise of well-bred absence of ostentation; but in a social economy geared to money, and not to any forceful aesthetic, the Puritan ideal must triumph.

When men are at war, their fashions tend to be plain—and thus, in most cases, reasonably becoming. With the return of peace, the fashions established by the necessities of war are modified to the uses of peaceful life. In the 17th century, however, it was not so much a question of the British Warm being worn with the rank-badges stripped off, but of badges of social rank, a multiplicity of ribands, being added to the plain fighting-dress of the Cromwellians, and the equally plain dress of the mercantile classes who backed the Divine Right of Parliament against the Divine Right of the King.

[1] My italics.

The advance of the Turks to the gates of Vienna, and the European wars of Louis XIV, which had taken his men, either as regular troops or as "volunteers" to the Eastern confines of Europe, had once again made the West preoccupied with the East. The activities of the various East India companies had brought in fabrics from India and China, and clothes were colourful. The French "volunteers" returned from Croatia with their sashes or lace-trimmed handkerchiefs knotted loosely around their throats—*à la cravate*—in the Croatian mode. Both the fashion and the name, *cravat*, survive. The "falling band" was displaced almost immediately by this elegantly-careless and pre-eminently comfortable fashion of covering the neck.

Hat with embryo "Kevenhuller" cock, 1690

It is at the end of the 17th century that the first effects of the military on fashion are seen. Troops who had fought abroad brought back odd hats, and the mercenaries of the period wore their characteristic national dress.

When it was decided to arm the dragoon with grenades, the first devised-for-the-job uniform cap in the British Army was introduced. Hitherto, all the men had worn the wide-brimmed, flat hat worn by civilians. Now, as it was inconvenient for a dragoon to throw a grenade whilst wearing a brimmed hat, a special hat for this branch of the service was designed. This was a cap with a pendant cloth bag, and was to be the prolific breeder, during the next century and a half, of military caps.

With the coming of the Prince of Orange to the throne, as co-Sovereign with Mary Stuart his cousin, uniform as we know it was introduced. If it was necessary to distinguish between friend and foe in the civil war, it was even more necessary to mark friends under William. William had brought his Dutch guards with him, and these foreigners had aroused all the never-very-latent xenophobia of the English. It was necessary to give all the King's men, foreigners and English alike, a distinctive uniform. The English made it quite clear that they would tolerate the Dutch only if they could not possibly be mistaken for them.

Dragoon farrier's fur cap, mid-18th cent.

One wonders what sort of hats were worn by "two hundred

Foot-Guard's cap, 1704 (front view)

Foot-Guard's cap, 1704 (side view)

Blacks brought from the Plantations of the Netherlands in America"; but though no details of the shape are given, it is clear that the Blacks had got away, like the British dragoons, from the once universal Quaker hat. The Blacks were dressed in "fur-lined embroidered caps ornamented with plumes of white feathers."

One of our allies at that time was the Duke of Courland, a Baltic state since absorbed into the vast Russian Empire.

The Duke commanded a regiment of Dragoons who were called "Finlanders or Laplanders in Bearskins taken from the wild Beasts they had slain, the common Habit of the cold Climate, with black armour and broad Flaming Swords." Carman calls attention to the oil-painting at Hampton Court which shows a body of these horsemen, in black uniforms, wearing fur-edged caps having long flying hoods.

These horsemen, whose equipment sounds as though it had been contributed equally by a Guardsman and the Archangel Michael, obviously bequeathed the use of bearskin to us: for this is the first mention that I find of it in the records of British military uniform.

Before the end of the century, proper distinction had been made between the various regiments in the matter of dress. Apart from special caps, such as those worn by the dragoons, the infantryman was put into the mitre or sugar-loaf cap, and the officers had their wide-brimmed hats turned up on three sides, with the edge of the brim laced: the famous Three-cornered Hat of the 18th century had arrived.

Armour was reintroduced in the campaigns of Marlborough against the French; and the cavalrymen of the Life Guards, shown in the wall-paintings on the Tarriers or Malplaquet Staircase at Marlborough House, wear three-cornered hats, laced with yellow or gold, according to rank.

Grenadiers in the service of foreign states wore fur caps at this period, but the British grenadiers wore caps of embroidered cloth until the middle of the 18th century. However, that there were exceptions to the rule is shown in the description of a deserter from Wynn's Regiment, quoted by Carman.

This particular soldier had a cap faced with bearskin, but the other members of his regiment had "red cloth caps faced with yellow and a wolf's head embroidered thereon."

Note here that, except in the case of the "Guards," these early regimental caps did not bear the Royal Arms or Cypher, but the crest or device of the Colonel of the Regiment.

When the fusil was introduced, this necessitated another change in headgear. Provided with a leather sling, the fusil could be slung over the shoulder; but, as the muzzle of the fusil got in the way of the hat-brim, the hat was replaced by a cap.

Foot-Guard's cap, 1704 (back view)

Other changes can mostly be related to the introduction either of new weapons or of new ways of employing older lethal aids.

Chapter Ten

WIGS OF THE 18TH CENTURY

WHEN Queen Anne came to the throne in 1702, the population of England and Wales was about 4,000,000. Exactly a century later, when the Peace of Amiens brought a temporary halt in the war between George III and the First Consul, the population of the country, excluding Scotland and Ireland, was some 16,000,000. The population had been quadrupled within the space of one hundred years.

With this almost inconceivable increase in population had come an equally inconceivable increase in wealth. Halfway through the war which began with the French revolution, the National Debt had risen to £700,000,000—and most of it had been spent in subsidizing Britain's allies. When the war which began with the revolt of the American Colonies ended in 1783, Britain calculated that she had lost 9,000 ships at sea in the course of a seven years' campaign. Nine years later, Britain had recovered sufficiently to go to war again—for twenty years.

All through the 18th century, Britain's wealth was increasing.

Yet, as the tendency was towards more and more personal and national wealth, the tendency of fashion was to ever-greater simplicity. The century began with full-bottomed wigs and gold-laced, feather-trimmed, three-cornered hats. It ended with the first "silk" top-hat, short, natural hair, brass-buttoned blue coats, plain breeches and hessians.

"Formal" wear, right up to the French Revolution, was "formal" indeed, to the point of folly. The vast, powdered coiffures worn by the women, with flowers and fruit, and even sailing ships atop, hardly argue a trend towards simplicity; but the simplicity had arrived in day-dress, both for men and women, long before the Revolution of 1789 made it

Cocked, 1695

134

Three-cornered, 1704

inadvisable to wear elaborate coiffures or even to powder the hair.

Before that final simplicity was reached, a simplicity always to be associated with Brummel, who made it fashionable, there were to be extravagances innumerable.

Yet the 18th century not unjustly prided itself on being an Age of Reason, despite the dress fantasies—centred about the hair and hat—of the Macaronis, the Merveilleuses, the Incroyables, there was an underlying sobriety in everything that the 18th century did and wore. There was nothing in that century of Marlborough and Pope, of Gay and Johnson, of Priestley and Washington, which even approached the fashions of the 1660s, in their vulgar fantasy (laced petticoat-breeches and the rest), and certainly never came within thinking distance of the age which had produced piked shoes and turbanhats with ground-reaching liripipes and suits hung with little bells. Only in one respect did a sartorial whimsy, both of the 15th and 16th centuries, come back into favour: that was in the pelisse of the Hussars, brought back at the very end of the century.

This fashion reminds one irresistibly, both of the hanging sleeves of the 15th century (and transmitted "traditionally" to later times), and the really curious and quite inexplicable fashion, encountered at the end of the 16th century, of wearing the short, loose, sleeved coat, called the Mandelion or Mandeville, "Colley-Westonwards." That is, the garment was "worn sideways, with the front and back panels draping the shoulders, while one sleeve hung down in front and the other behind." This lunatic fashion belongs to a well-known and periodically recurrent passion for putting a familiar garment on "Colley-Westonwards," or awry. The hat-turban, as we have seen, developed from the liripiped hood's being put on in a similar "Colley-Westonwards" way.

One point to notice in the history of fashion is that much of the evidence is adduced from fashion-plates: that is to say, from the pictures of the richer classes, dressed in their richest garments.

Only occasionally did the fancy take the distinguished sitter to commission the artist to show him or her in plain, workaday clothes; but when this happens, we are struck by the "modernity" of the garments.   They not only do not seem "fancy dress" but we realize, with something of a shock, that, so dressed, the wearer of these simple, practical garments could walk down the street and hardly be noticed for an unusual sight.   Take the famous portrait of Lord Stafford in the National Portrait Gallery: he is dressed for shooting.   He wears a short, single-breasted jacket, and ankle length trousers. Only the material of which the suit is made—a striped "pyjama-like" cloth—is unusual.   But when we say that his lordship seems to be dressed in a pair of pyjamas, we realize how very simple the clothes of even the most over-dressed periods could be, away from formality and the artist who records only that formality.

Just so with the 18th century: the fops and dandies were recorded, but sufficient of the other sort of men were recorded, too, to let us see how plainly a man, apart from ball or Court, could dress.

The difference, indeed, between day-dress and "dress clothes" was every bit as marked in the 18th century as it is today: but the difference was no greater.   Plain cloth, often unpowdered hair or the plainest of wigs: that by day.   At night, rich materials, embroidered, tinselled, spangled: yes, but the cut rarely less plain than that of the sober working clothes.

The Wig has been extensively surveyed throughout its entire near-two-century-long history.   The contemporary names have been listed, and names supplied where the originals have been forgotten.

Military, 1742

Thus, we have the Campaign, the Full-bottomed, the Ramillies, the Long Bob, the Short Bob, the Full Bob, the Night-Cap, the Scratch, the Cut, the Natural, the Tye, the Caxon, the Spencer, the Adonis and all the rest of the wigs. But I have never seen it noticed that the shapes of the various wigs in use during the 18th century correspond too closely for the resemblance to be accidental to the shapes of the coifs and cauls and undercaps and English and French hoods with which heads were covered in the pre-Wig ages. A suggestion which may account for this shape-resemblance is that the wig was originally built up on a cap of traditional shape.

In the years before the Civil War, there was a fashion for a "love lock" among the smart young fellows and the vain old codgers. The hair at the back was permitted to grow long, and this was twisted into a "love lock," which was brought over the shoulder, and fastened to the breast by means of a silken bow.

Surely the pig-tail queue is nothing but the somewhat formalized inheritor of the "love lock's" decease?

Let us briefly look at the differences among wigs.

The full-bottomed wig, still worn by the Speaker of the House of Commons, the Lord Chancellor and other high dignitaries, was fashionable until about 1730, afterwards being reserved to those classes who tend to keep fashions alive beyond their natural period of life. At first, the full-bottomed wig was "horned"; the curls being arranged into peaks either side the centre parting—a fashion owing its inspiration to the women's Fontange or, it may be, the other way around?

Full-bottomed wig, general type

After Queen Anne's death, the "horns" were flattened, and in about 1720, the "lappets" were not only shortened, but allowed to fall behind the shoulders. The origin of the present full-bottomed wig is therefore seen to be at some time before 1720.

A full-bottomed wig could cost some £20, in 1705: a price which, as we shall see, not only tended to produce the smaller and cheaper wig, but produced a numerous array of wigs made of substitute materials.

The Campaign or Travelling wig was a bushy wig, enclosing the face like a hood, with a centre parting, and three tails. Worn by travellers, hence the name. It was favoured by elderly men, and did not go out of fashion until after the mid-century.

The Bob was an all-purpose wig, worn by all classes in "undress." If it covered the neck, it was called a Long Bob; if not, the Short Bob. Someone with an historical memory must have been responsible for naming the short-haired style of hairdressing introduced by Irene Castle in 1915: the Bob.

Until about 1750, the Bob had a centre parting: after that, the hair was "brushed back" without parting. The hair at the back was either curled in a tight roll (or rolls) or waved in a neat fringe. Long Bobs were sometimes tied with a ribbon at the back.

The Night-Cap was a Short Bob, with several roll-curls framing the back of the head, and stretching from cheek to cheek.

Full Bobs—or Ministers' Bobs—were very bushy, being frizzed and not curled.

Scratch wig was the wig reduced to its minimum size for convenience: it was the favourite wig of all busy men; sportsmen, clergymen, tradesmen: it was introduced about 1740, and gave a neat, practical appearance to the head. The Cut wig was also a small, plain affair, and was worn by artisans, lesser tradesmen, clerks and, in a higher social category, riders.

The wig fashion touched an element of the preposterous in the Natural wig, which was a wig carefully imitating the natural hair.

In any other age, the Natural wig would have seemed reasonable: a sop to the vanity of the bald. But the wig in the 18th century was intended to be artificial in appearance: so that to contrive one to look natural seems absurd. There is reason to believe, though, that they were very much cheaper than the other types of wig—"Mr Cowper had a very light natural wig for 28/." (1718—quoted by Cunnington.)

Called, by those who wore them, Perukes and Periwigs, as well as Wigs, these head-coverings, which were worn by all classes save the farm-labourer, the common sailor and the despairing poor in the rat-holes of St Giles's, were, like most universal fashions, highly susceptible of modifications to express the individual fancy.

The more subtle of these modifications necessarily escape us, but to the 18th century the cut of a man's wig was as indicative of his character as, to us, is the cult and tilt of his hat; the choice of his necktie.

Up to about 1735, the Front Hair was given a parting; from about 1730, the Toupee or Foretop came in, a style of hair-dressing in which the hair was brushed back to form a narrow roll above the temples.

Sometimes the wearer's own hair was permitted to grow in front; this was then combed down over the face, the (frontless) wig put in position, and the natural hair combed up and back over the forward edge of the toupee, with whose hair the natural hair was blended by means of bear's grease.

A linen wrapper put over the shoulders, powder was then sprayed over the whole head, natural and artificial hair alike, so that neither was distinguishable from the other. This powder could be white, but was often of that shade of blue which has given the name, *Powder Blue*, to a certain shade of cloth. Count Pamphili, of the Austrian Legation, who was living in Princes' Gate in the early 1930s, invariably ordered his liveried footmen to powder their natural hair with powder of this blue shade.

Theatrical and cinematograph producers have, as a safety measure, evolved what we may call a "standard 18th century type" of wig, that is, with the hair brushed back from the forehead, two banks of cylindrical curls over each ear, a queue, and generally a black satin bow at the top of the queue, in the style favoured by senior schoolgirls and junior lady-clerks up to about 1916.

Accordingly, this type of wig—almost identical with the present day barrister's wig[1]—has become familiar to all who, in Norman Douglas's phrase, "frequent picture palaces."

It is a type which, though widely used in the 18th century, did not come in until about the middle of the century. The development was through the frizzing of the hair at the sides, and leaving it to hang down in front of the ears—the ears and the neck behind being left uncovered. The 18th century, despite its sudden passion for the Rococo—associated with the names of such designers as Halfpenny, Ince, Mayhew, Mainwaring and Chippendale—preferred "neatness," and the fuzzy-wuzzy style of dressing the side hair gave way to the

[1] The Serjeants-at-Law wore a black patch on the crown of their wigs.

neater style of dressing the side hair in horizontal rolls, which might be continued right around the back of the wig.   The uncurled wig survives as the formal head-covering both of County Court judges and judges of the Appeal Court.   It is interesting to know that Progress has not left even these venerable relics of antiquity untouched: the use of horsehair is being discontinued, and the new wigs are being made of nylon —"Easily cleaned, sir, and very much lighter than the old horsehair wigs for wear in tropical climates."

The Tye wig, favoured by undergraduates and as "off-duty" wear by men ordinarily given to wearing the more formal types, was as its name implies, a wig in which the curls were drawn back, and tied together with a ribbon:—"The smart tye wig with the black ribbon shows a man of fierceness of temper."

Club wig, general type   Cunnington notes that the large tye wig was often extremely bushy, and quotes Horace Walpole's description of his interview with Lord Sandwich at the Admiralty:

"I could have no hope of getting at his ear, for he has put on such a first-rate tye-wig that nothing without the lungs of a boatswain can even think to penetrate the thickness of the curls."   (*Letters*, 1745.)

A curious commentary on this typical flight of Walpolian fancy is the little-known Hogarth painting, dating probably from the same year in which the Walpole letter was written. Hogarth's "conversation piece" is set in the comfortably furnished captain's cabin of a first-rate man-o'-war.   The group shows Lord George Graham, with his purser, chaplain, cook, black servant and dog.

There is another dog—type unascertainable—which is mounting guard over an enormous Famille Rose punch-bowl, brimming with liquor, which is at the chaplain's feet.   Whatever Smollet wrote about conditions at sea in the 18th century, the officers suffered few discomforts!

The different ways of dealing with the head are interesting and instructive.   The cook has a loose white woollen cap, the chaplain has a "Natural" wig, the purser wears his own curly hair, unpowdered, the black servant has a sort of Scots bonnet of vaguely Oriental flavour, worn with a decided tilt, Lord George wears a loose velvet, tasselled cap—and the King Charles's spaniel, sitting up on its hunkers, is wearing the captain's full-bottomed wig. Out of the Admiralty, Lord Sandwich, too, would have been as prompt to discard his ear-stopping tye-wig.

The Pig-tail, though "informal," was considered very elegant. It has a small "crown" and long queue, the "pig-tail" being either twisted with ribbon or spirally bound with it. Bows were tied at each end of the queue.

The Ramillies, hence its name, was worn by Guards officers, and by young fellows affecting a military air. It had a queue which diminished to a point from a fairly wide top and either one or two black silk bows were worn on the queue.

The undress Caxon tye-wig was always a blond or white one.

References to wigs are, naturally, plentiful throughout the literature of the 18th century, though the references are not always intelligible to us now. For instance, the Spencer wig that Smollet mentions in Roderick Random cannot now be identified, any more than can the Adonis, mentioned (1754) in the *London Magazine or Gentleman's Monthly Intelligencer*: "I have seen a prim young fellow with a Cur or Adonis, as they call the effeminate Wigs of the present Vogue, plaister'd rather than powder'd, and appearing like the twigs of a gooseberry bush in a deep snow."

That the name, "Adonis," was not invented by the writer in *The London Magazine* is apparent from a quotation of later date—1775—in which the Adonis is mentioned as "a fine flowing . . . or white periwig."

Obviously, when "everyone" wore a wig—"It's better to be out of the world than out of the fashion," said Colley Cibber, himself a wig-wearer—and human hair was vastly expensive: "For a tied wig £7 1s." (1754): cheaper substitutes had to be used to keep a population of many millions supplied with these indispensable head-coverings.

The most obvious substitute for human hair was horse-hair

—still used: "A fine horsehair wig £2 10s." (1725); but the other substitutes seem so incredible to us that their employment must testify to the inescapableness of this fashion.

Goat's hair seems reasonable, but do feathers?—and yet wigs made of feathers were favoured by parsons.

Contemporary advertisements give some hint of the "source of raw materials" for these feathered wigs—"the Parson's feather-top frizzed broad and high (1775)"—mallards' and drakes' tails are mentioned.

Cork wigs were also advertised "either smooth or in curls."

Certainly the most extraordinary substitute for hair in wig-making was wire. Copper and iron wire, in "watch spring" curls were worn from about 1750 to about 1770. They were known as Iron or Wire wigs, and that fastidious man Horace Walpole was sufficiently pleased with their appearance to write in 1751, to Sir Horace Mann, telling him of the iron wig that he had brought from Paris—"you literally would not know it from hair."

After that, the use of thread, silk, worsted, mohair seems perfectly natural.

There was a brief interlude in this fashion of wig-wearing about 1765, when many of the younger men began to wear their own hair.

The peruke-makers, threatened with ruin, promptly petitioned the King to order the smart young fellows back into wigs.

As the first half of the century ended, it was seen that wigs tended to become classified according to social rank and profession.

The full-bottomed wig had been reserved for the upper brackets of the Law and the Church; the Bob wig, small, with several rows of curls (the modern barrister's wig) became fashionable around mid-century, and stayed in use until the last decade of the century. The Full-dress Bob, costing about thirty shillings or a guinea-and-a-half, came into fashion in the 1760s.

The Scratch Bob combined false and natural hair, so that it covered only the back of the head, the natural hair being

"Montem" mitre, worn at Eton, late 18th cent.

brought up, and brushed over the wig, to which it was united by pomatum. It was often "natural" in colour to match the wearer's hair.

The Scratch Bob was associated with horsemen, parsons and those who either took a lot of exercise or were not rich enough to afford the more elaborate wigs.

Learned professions, particularly the medical, favoured the Physical wig from about 1750 onwards. Replacing the full-bottomed wig, the Physical was like a larger Long Bob. With or without a parting, it stood out around the head, often hanging down below the nape of the neck: "What wags call a lion or a pompey." Joshua Reynolds's famous portrait of Doctor Johnson—given immortality by being used as an advertisement for beer—shows the Doctor wearing a peculiarly fine example of the Physical wig. When worn by physicians, the Physical wigs were larger than those of others.

Cut wigs were, as the name suggests, "utility" wigs, worn by the working classes. They were short and never curled; nor powdered, either.

Cavalryman's campaign hat, 1742

The tendency, with queued wigs, was to make them smaller and with fewer curls. The curls, which were formed by bending the hair around a pipe-clay former, were usually called "buckles," from the French, *bouclé*. A "buckled wig," then, means not a wig fastened with a buckle, but one provided with curls. "Dildo" was another name for a wig curl.

Other names for wigs, as the century passes on from 1750 to 1790; at which date all but the professions, the elderly and the conservative had abandoned the wig; are fairly self-explanatory.

The Pigeon-winged toupee (1750–1770), the Greque—"The hair is dressed in two long curls on each side, and a Grecque behind like a horseshoe. It is tied behind in a long tail à la Panurge" (1787)—the Bag wig, worn for dress and full-dress, had either a stiff satin bow or a silk rosette at the back. The large bag was worn in the 1770s.

The Catogan or Club wig was one with a thick, flat queue, folded and tied back on itself with ribbon. The Macaronis favoured this type in the 1770s—though theirs was always

5th Dragoon Guards,
Officer, *1800*

larger than the Catogans of less foppish men.   It was an undress wig.

The Major was a military wig, resembling a Bob, with two corkscrew curls, tied together at the nape of the neck to form a two-pronged queue behind.   Popular during the three decades, 1750–1780, it was also worn, like all other fashions associated with the military, by civilians.   The French name for the double-queued wig was the Brigadier, and this name was also used in England.

This raises another point in considering the fashions of the 18th century: we have mentioned that the origin of the all-European wig-wearing fashion was undoubtedly French.   This influence of the French on European fashion continued, in undiminished force, throughout the 18th century, in spite of the fact that England and France were so often at war, declared or undeclared.

The white or blond Caxon continued to be worn; but, under the influence of the philosophy which lay behind such impractical dreamings as Rousseau's *Contrat Social* and Marie Antoinette's dairy-farm at the Little Trianon, a fashion appeared in the 1780s for wearing a wig dressed in "a natural disorder."   The hair hung long and loose, and was neither curled nor tied.   This style was called the Peruke Naissante or *à l'Enfant*.   As a new style of wig, it was perhaps the last to be introduced before the wig itself vanished for ever from civilian and lay dress.

It is said that Pitt killed the wig when, in 1795, he introduced his tax of a guinea a year on the use of hair-powder.   Unlike some other laws, this was enforced: two cases being recorded, in 1797, where the offenders were fined each ten guineas with costs.   He had taxed hats in 1785—unsuccessfully.

The wig at this time had reached its final, and highly practical, form: a tightly brushed back toupee, with a stiff roll-curl above each ear, and a short, tight pig-tail.   Exemptions were granted from the tax to certain professions; but those who, having no right to exemption, paid up their guinea, were known contemptuously as "guinea pigs," a derisive phrase which survives in reference to those decorative nobodies who adorn the boards of public companies, in return for directors' fees.

To say that the 18th century women did not adopt the male fashion of the wig needs some explanation. Women wore false hair, but wore it in conjunction with their own: they did *not* shave their heads, and cover the shaven crowns with wigs.

But, as the century drew to a close, they puffed up the hair with pads and false rolls and curls of false hair. They "stuffed" their coiffures with tow or horsehair, as a cushion is stuffed, drawing the hair over it. Flowers and fruit, as well as feathers and other trimmings became increasingly common, and though the "ship in full sail" fashion was a French one, confined to only a few, the hairdressing of the smart English-woman, in the 1770s and 1780s, was elaborate enough.

Where whole wigs were worn, they were worn over the natural hair. Powder came in in the latter part of the century: it appears to have originated with Court dress. It continued even after the elaborate, towering coiffures had gone out with the Revolution and it enhanced the charm of the "cropped hair" styles, immediately post-Revolution, which were cynically called "à la guillotine."

Chapter Eleven

SIMPLICITY AND ELEGANCE IN THE 18TH CENTURY

Women's hats and head-dressing began simply in the Fontange or the lace or linen cap, and, except for the elaborate styles of hairdressing favoured in the period just before the Revolution, women's fashions, during the 18th century, are marked by simplicity and good taste.

Whether or not the cap—now very small—covered the top of the head or not, it was always worn: both indoors and out (under a hat or walking-hood). The use of lace for these small head-coverings—the 18th century term for any head-dress was a "head"—could make the cap very expensive indeed: a "head" of Brussels lace cost £40 in 1709. The Fontange, which went out a little before the end of Queen Anne's reign, was replaced by the Round-eared Cap, which was sometimes called a coif. This remained in fashion until the late 1760s, but it had a number of other caps to rival it.

For undress, women used the Mob Cap; but there were variants on both of these, the variations tending either to hide the head or to reveal it.

Widows wore the Bandore and Peak, a term remembered in our calling hair which dips towards the eyes, a "widow's peak."

The Bandore and Peak was a black band, with peak, and a veil, also black, hanging down behind. This style of head-dress is still to be seen abroad, especially at royal funerals.

Hoods were worn out of doors: the hood attached to a cloak, the so-called long hood, with ends which crossed over the breast, the Short or Pug-hood, tied under the chin, the Caped Hood, gathered round the neck, and spreading out in a single or double collar over the shoulders, the Riding Hood or Capuchin, deep-caped and often with a coloured lining: all these were worn throughout the century.

Hats were usually worn over caps, and were in general strongly influenced in style by the contemporary male mode. Felt, silk and straw were used, and hats could be Small, Slouch, Bergère (the large, flat French straw hat), Witch's; fashionable only for a short while in the 1740s, and then becoming a hat for countrywomen; Three-cornered and Jockey, this last for riding or country-wear. Mostly made of velvet, it was often adorned, not only with a feather, but with a fringe of false curls as well.

After 1760, the caps and hats worn by women tended to become larger: the caps being goffered and being cut to conceal the ears and cheeks. Bright, wide ribbons, usually blue or pink, were used as "hat-bands" on the caps: again, we see the influence of the French mode.

There were the Pulteney cap, round-eared and worn mostly by the elderly (Martha Washington can be seen in a fine Pulteney); the Ranelagh Mob, which was a handkerchief folded diagonally and tied under the chin; the Joan or Quaker Cap, which was a "baby's bonnet," or, in other words, our old friend, the Coif; the Dormeuse or French Night-cap, resembling somewhat the Dutch bonnet. It must be remembered that, as the natural hair, which had been worn unadorned throughout the first six decades of the 18th century, became more and more enriched with false hair, pads, and other aids to luxuriance, the caps to cover it necessarily increased in size.

All the above caps were "undress." But there were "dress" caps, too, of which the most enchanting was the Butterfly: a small lace cap, wired up into a butterfly-shape, and worn above the forehead. For Court wear, frilled lappets were added, and the hair further adorned with jewelled and other trimming.

Fantastic styles, though not common, and lasting only a short while, are encountered: among these may be mentioned the short-lived Cabriole or Caprioll head-dress—"All that we hear from France is that a new madness reigns there," writes Horace Walpole in 1754.

The "new madness" was for hats to be replaced by

lightweight models of cabrioles or other carriages, made of gold wire and drawn by horses of blown glass.

The Turban was worn both for dress and undress; but there were simple fashions, too, such as that which consisted only of a puff of gauze on the head, from which a long streamer fell.

For practical outdoor wear, the most striking was the Calash; a folding hood built up of silk on arches of split cane. This folded like the hood of a pre-war car, and appears to be the predecessor of the Gibus or crush- or opera-hat of the mid-19th century. The Calash covered the head completely, shielding the face both from the weather and from the insolent gaze of the vulgar. Bonnets, Bergère or Milkmaid hats, the small forward-tilted hat made familiar to us by Phiz's drawing of Dolly Varden: all these hats of the post-1760 period gradually enlarged until, by 1790, though still preserving their original shape, they had become twice or three times the size. It was to take the French Revolution to introduce the cap once more: but, for reasons of sheer fright, as well as because all the refugees were necessarily non-Republicans, the English ladies hung on to pre-Revolution fashions until the very end of the 18th century, and even a little way beyond.

The styles of the late 18th century, and the early years of the 19th century are marked by a most elegant simplicity. Obsessed with a "classical" rationalization of their revolutionary principles, the French rulers made anything Greek or Roman fashionable; and dress, no less than furniture, reflected this preoccupation with the golden ages of Republican Greece and Republican Rome.

The attempt to translate Greek and Roman fashions into an acceptable modern idiom produced results which, though hardly classical, were undeniably charming, and are summed up at their most elegant in David's famous portrait of Madame Recamier reclining on a sofa.

Wide-brimmed hat, c. 1800

The curious thing is, that though the English of the upper and more prosperous middle classes might not have liked the French republicans, the reverse was very far from true. The simplicity of the ordinary dress, both of Englishmen and

Englishwomen, had struck the French republicans as being an ideal example for republicans to copy. Under the influence of such artists as Carle Vernet, English sports and English clothes had been introduced to France. Voltaire had long before introduced the ideas of English "democratic" principles and the Anglophilia which had been the characteristic of fashionable Frenchmen prior to the Revolution survived that great social change. The French republicans were as Anglophile—at least in matters of dress—as the men of Versailles. The odd thing is that the English, to judge by contemporary references to French fashions, did not know that they were importing their own styles.

Dragoon's, 1742

For men, too, the century ended in a simplicity with which it had not begun; though, to be sure, the styles of 1700 were marked by a striking contrast from those of 1665. Simplicity was on its inevitable way, even in 1700.

The style, as we have said, which is most characteristic of the 18th century, is the Cocked or Three-cornered Hat, or rather the Cocking of the Wide-brimmed Hat. Strictly speaking, the phrase "Cocked" is not synonymous with "Three-cornered," for as we shall see it is possible to cock the hat with one, two, three or even four flaps. Talking of "cocking," which came in long before William III's reign (the cocking of the hat seems to distinguish between officers and men in the Philip Sidney engraving of 1585) reminds us of William Coke, supposed inventor of the "Billycock," a supposed corruption of "Billy Coke."

Let us examine the legend which attributes the invention of the Billycock to this eminent scientific agriculturalist. First of all, take his name: Thomas William Coke, born 1752, died 1842; created Earl of Leicester of Holkham, 1837. There is no record that he was ever called, either by his cronies or by the mob, anything other than "Tom." Whence the "Billy"?

The only famous "Billy" of that time was William, Duke of Clarence, afterwards King William IV, who was affectionately known (affectionately, because Prince William was a sailor at a time when the Navy could do no wrong) as "Silly Billy."

Fusilier's cap, 1710

Another famous "Billy" of the time was Stephenson's locomotive, "Puffing Billy"—but no one yet has associated the steam-engine with the hat, though the shape of the condenser on a steam-locomotive does resemble a billycock.

On the other hand, we find, at the beginning of the 18th century, the term, used of a hat-style, "bully cocked," almost certainly meaning, according to Murray, "cocked after the fashion of the bullies, or hectoring blades of the period." Murray adds that "billy cock" is "a colloquial term for a round, low-crowned felt hat worn by men, and sometimes also by young women."

That this is the explanation of the origin of "Billycock" seems certain; especially when we consider how often reference is made, particularly in the early part of the 18th century, to the social and emotional significances of various types of "cocking."

Turning the brim up high, all the way round, was recorded as "the fierce trooper's cock"; pinching the front of the three-cornered hat, to give a sharp point—another military style—was known as the "Kevenhuller cock," and a hat so cocked was known as a "Kevenhuller hat."

Throughout the 18th century, the differences, though significant at the time both to those who wore the hats and to the hatters who sold them, seem to us to resolve themselves into two classes: the change in the hat's size, and the change in the hat's *position* on the head, i.e., whether the "peak" was worn to the front or to the side, and so on. When the two-flapped hats were introduced from France, and became fashionable at the end of the century, the position had to be altered, so as not to accord with Republican usage.

The size varied more than the mode of wearing the hat: small until the coming of George I, then larger, then small again from about 1730. Then, from 1740, as the century wore on, the tendency was to wear the hat smaller, except for the strange military styles in the end-of-century reaction, when the two-flapped hats of the generals and staff officers in all countries assumed literally monstrous proportions.

1st Life Guards, Officer, 1812

Sometimes the hat was made small for another reason: so

that it might be carried under the arm—a "chapeau bras," though the hat designed to be carried *only* under the arm was not introduced until the 1770s.

Mrs Centlivre has an interesting comment on hat-manners in *The Stolen Heiress*; "Your beaux wear their hats thus (clapping it under his arm); your conceited wits thus (putting it over the left eye); your country squire thus (putting it behind his wig)."

Marine's cap, 1742

That was written in 1700: it more or less applied throughout the century.

The Monmouth Cock, referred to in writings of the period, was the manner of wearing the hat with only the back turned up. It was regarded as old-fashioned even at the beginning of the century, and is mostly seen in the portraits only of cranks, usually misers.

All the old materials were used in hat-making, but felt and beaver were the most sought after. Straw hats were worn in the warmer weather, and "nightcaps" were worn indoors by those who had put off their wigs, or by artisans at their work.

A word now about the uniforms which came into general use in this century. The three-cornered hat, with the forward "pinch" not quite centred, but turned a little to the left, was worn by all troops except those who wore the dragoon cap of fur-trimmed cloth (with a bag) and the fusilier's mitre. The Marines also wore a cap, not unlike the fusilier's mitre, but not as tall and with a rounded top.

Scots infantryman, 1742

The Scots regiments wore the flat bonnet, with a red "pom-pom" on top, and a feather stuck in at what seems to be a right angle to the edge of the cap.

After the turn of the half-century, the headwear of all the troops, save only the dragoons, were standardized as the three-cornered hat, which meant that, in order to achieve individuality in units, the Colonels devised a hundred different ways of wearing the three-cornered hats. It was from this search for novelty that the two-flapped hat—what the French still call the "bicorne"—evolved. And the "bicorne" itself could be worn either "thwartships" or "fore-and-aft." The Guards

Militia, 1778

Contemporary French drawing of "revolutionary" Phrygian bonnet, c. 1790

officers in 1756 introduced, as we have seen, the 15th–16th century fashion of slashing the brim, which was turned up in front and not at the sides.

Naval officers did not get an official uniform until 1756; the matloe not until exactly a century later. But officers already wore the civilian cocked hat, and continued to wear it until it changed into the familiar "naval cocked hat" at the beginning of the 19th century. The ordinary seamen wore it, too, as is shown by this 18th century description of a Jack Tar, which shows him as having been dressed in, "A little low cocked hat, a pea-jacket (a sort of cumbrous Dutch-cut coat), a pair of petticoat trousers, not unlike a Scotch kilt, tight stockings and shoes with pinchbeck buckles."

But Jack also wore his traditional and ancient stocking-cap, and, at the end of the century, the flat-brimmed, squared-off-topped "boater," either of straw, usually varnished, or of tarred canvas or leather.

A contemporary picture, *The Sailor's Return*, showing one of Anson's officers greeting his wife (or sweetheart) makes it clear that the dress of naval officers at that time—1744—was indistinguishable from that of civilians. The officer, however, wears his hat with two "pinches" at each side of the head, the third "pinch" being at the back.

2nd Foot Guards, Officer, 1792

In the Print Room at the British Museum, there is a most interesting watercolour drawing (not a very good one) of an Hussar: blue and yellow uniform, complete with pelisse, peakless tall shako, with bag and plume, tight breeches and hessians, sabre and sabre-tache.

The date of this drawing is 1784, the artist who painted it was George, Prince of Wales,[1] and its interest for us lies in the fact that this drawing of a uniform that George proposed to wear to a fancy dress ball (he was twenty at the time) shows that even at an early age, the future Prince Regent and King had the idea of putting the whole British Army into colourful uniforms, with special emphasis on their military headgear.

As the French Revolutionary Armies went triumphantly

[1] Print Room, British Museum, Reference No. 1857-5-20-87.

across Europe, they collected, not only allies from distant parts, but also the uniforms peculiar to those allies.

Napoleon collected more; and the uniforms appealed not only to the French, but to their many enemies. Particularly did the uniform of the Polish lancers and the Hungarian hussars appeal to the military minds of most of Europe. Colonels began to put their men into the modified version of these uniforms, and though the rank-and-file Guards' "grenadier" caps had been converted into bearskins with a brass plate in front, above the edge of the cap, the other regiments were mostly in three-cornered hats. The Guards officers still wore the "two-cornered" hat, with the flaps turned up back and front.

East India Company Officer's bearskin, 1799

Hussars were formed out of the Light Dragoons in 1805, and given what they and the Prince had long sanctioned "unofficially:" the complete Hussar outfit, while the remaining Light Dragoons gave themselves a uniform very Hussarish in cut, with fur shako, crimson bag and plume, the whole being secured to the tunic by a spirally wound length of gold cord.

In 1800, the Prince of Wales's Own Regiment of Light Dragoons were put into a new form of dragoon cap, a peaked affair with a great crest of fur. For all the cavalry, the Prince revived that archaic and discontinued accessory, the sabre-tache.

The straight-sided shako was introduced for such regiments as the Highland Infantry and the Rifle Regiments, formed out of such émigré troops as the Royal American Regiment of Foot, Hompesch's Mounted Riflemen and Lowenstein's Chasseurs.

Before the end of the Napoleonic Wars, the straight-sided "English" shako had been replaced by the uniform-conscious Prince to the bell-topped "French" shako.

The sailor had already adopted what was to be his official uniform, though the merchant sailor apparently continued to use the 17th century petticoat-breeches until at least as late as the 1830s.

The Royal Marines at Trafalgar must have been in what

18th Hussars, Officer, 1812

Rifle Corps, Officer, 1812

was then the "very latest": "silk" toppers, decorated with a cockade.

This brings us to the great hat-invention which marked the last years of the 18th century: the silk hat.

It was in 1797 that John Hetherington, a hatter doing business in Charing Cross, a few doors from Northumberland House, thought of making a tall hat—they had been "in" among the younger or more "republican" men since the 1780s and women had been wearing the feminine version of them for ten years—out of very fine silk shag: what we now call "hatter's plush."

The 18th century mob must have been an easy one to excite: so thick was the crowd which gathered around John Hetherington, as he stepped into Whitehall, with his silk hat shining in the sun, that the usual 18th century riot developed, in the course of which an errand boy broke his leg.

This was, though neither Hetherington nor the mob knew it, to be one of the world-conquerors among hats. The 18th century knew the round hat—they called it a "slouch" hat— but it failed to establish itself in fashion: it had to wait until the next century to achieve that—"I never admired a round hat, but with a large wig it is insupportable" (1787). The tall hat, the topper, was to conquer; to be *the* hat, par excellence, for more than a century.

Before we take leave of the 18th century, we must notice the disappearance of an ancient hat: the Cap of Maintenance or of Estate.

This cap, a "Robin Hood," with crimson crown, lined with ermine, and with ermine covering the turned up brim, was the symbol of sovereignty in the late Middle Ages.

"Round" hat, end of 18th cent.

At the coronation of an English, later British, sovereign, after the loss of England's French dominions, it was the custom for two men to walk in procession behind the sovereign, the men representing the Dukes of Aquitaine and Normandy, to which duchies the British Crown laid claim until the claim was abandoned under the Treaty of Amiens, in 1801.

Dressed in the impressive robes of sovereign dukes—they wore crimson velvet, trimmed with miniver—and taking precedence even of the royal dukes, the two men, usually actors, had their trains carried by pages, and in front of each marched a page, carrying, on a crimson velvet cushion trimmed with gold bullion, the Cap of Maintenance.

The coronation of George III was the last at which this picturesque survival was seen. With it went the Cap of Maintenance.

French shako, 1815

Chapter Twelve

TOP-HATTED CENTURY

Beaver, 1809

IF the 18th century was the century of the three-cornered hat, the century which succeeded it was, without doubt, the century of the top-hat. But, as the 19th century dawned with the top-hat not yet the sole permissible form of headwear among even fashionable men, so the 19th century closed with the top-hat's supremacy—its virtual universality —gravely challenged by the "soft felt, the Homburg and the 'hard felt'," the Bowler. It was not for another quarter century that young men—who make the fashions—were finally to abandon the top-hat save for ritual wear (weddings, race-meetings and funerals), but the supremacy of the top-hat ended with the 19th century, and it ended because the frock-coat was supplanted by the short jacket. Members of the Stock Exchange today wear the top-hat with the short jacket, but there the top-hat is worn ritually. When it was worn as a part of everyday dress, it needed the frock-coat to "balance" it. When the hitherto "informal" short jacket was adopted for more or less formal occasions, the equally "informal" homburgs and bowlers were admitted, too, to more or less formal wear. That, in the subconscious mind, the top-hat "went" with the frock-coat or morning-coat is shown by the sneers provoked when Mussolini wore a bowler with a morning-coat.

About the middle of the 19th century, as Mayhew's pictures show, every class wore the top-hat: peers, clerks, old-clothes-men—everybody who wore a hat at all. And, during the first half of the century, the uniformed officials, police, postmen, railway servants, wore the top-hat as well. Save that their headwear was brimless, with or without a peak, the military wore top-hats—or, at least, tall hats—too. But, at Trafalgar, the Marines wore actual top-hats, of hatter's plush, provided with the authentic curly brim, and made "uniform" only by the cockade at the side, of the fashion still worn by Royal

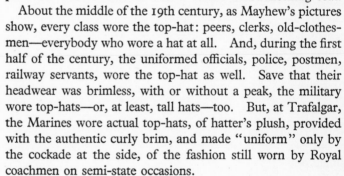

Light Infantry, Officer,
1848

coachmen on semi-state occasions.

156

The coming of the top-hat, of course, made the three-cornered hat an immediate object of regard by those of a "traditional" and ritualistic turn of mind. By being so thoroughly and so quickly outmoded, the three-cornered hat became ideal as a symbol of antiquity.

Lord Mayors and their coachmen, beadles, town-criers, Bank of England servants, Chelsea pensioners and similar "protected" groups were assured of the continuity as a ritual head-dress of what formerly had been the everyday wear of everyone—officials and civilians alike.

Three-cornered hat, end of 18th cent.

The top-hat conquered all other forms of headwear; to such an extent, indeed, that by the 1850s, the Birmingham japanners were manufacturing japanned *papier-mâché* top-hats, for those who could not run to the few shillings—or even pence—needed to buy a second-hand "topper."

Perhaps it is true that the challenge to the universality of the top-hat came, not from the fact that there were other fairly popular types of hat surviving or reintroduced from earlier centuries—the Billycock, the Wide Awake, the soft felt hat with floppy brim, what is called at Eton, a "Land and Water"—but that a large class of top-hat wearers, uniformed public servants, were taken out of their top-hats and put into semi-military peaked caps. When the first official issue of uniform to post-office letter-carriers was made in 1793—"because of the ragged condition of the carriers' own clothes"—the "issue hat" was a tall beaver; and this continued to be worn until 1859, when the beaver was replaced by the hard felt hat (a sort of high, flat-topped bowler), and this again was replaced, in 1862, by the single-peaked shako, called, by two official post-office historians, Messrs F. G. Raynham and W. S. G. Calvert, "the military peaked cap." Slight changes took place in this shako, modelled on that worn by contemporary French and American troops, but it remained in use until 1898, when it was replaced by the double-peaked shako, with a japanned leather peak in front and a cloth-covered peak at the back. This was replaced, in 1932, by the now universal single-peaked cap, of the newer military fashion.

Light Infantry, 1860

Three years after the postmen lost their top-hats, and were

New York policeman's
helmet, c. 1890

put into what *Punch* bitterly denounced a militaristic head-wear, the police lost *their* top-hats, and were given the "Ro-man" type of helmet which, with slight modifications, survives to this day. (It is of interest here to note that, when a questionnaire was sent out to members of the Lincolnshire Constabulary in 1958, asking the members what they thought of the new flat-topped, peaked caps, which had supplanted the old "Roman" helmet, the men, by an overwhelming vote, demanded their old helmets back. "The helmets," they said, "gave them more authority," i.e., distinguished them from the countless other peaked-cap wearers.)

The distribution of the helmets was curious: constables wore them, and so did Chief Constables—on official occasions they still do; but for the senior ranks above sergeant and below that of Chief Constable, the officers were issued with peaked pill-box caps, identical with the pattern then used for station-masters and merchant-marine officers. Caps of this old pattern are still worn by officials of the Royal Courts of Justice (the "Law Courts").

But let us go back to the beginning of the 19th century, when the top-hat, as we know it, had been introduced only two years: John Hetherington having made his first top-hat in hatter's plush, or "silk shag," in 1798. The tall hat, of "beaver," was, of course, a top-hat, but not the top-hat that we know and use today: that was Hetherington's invention, and it did not fully supplant the beaver until about 1860.

The tall hat, in fact, had come in, among the younger men, about 1780, and had supplanted the three-cornered hat, among the younger men, by 1790. The influence of the French Revolution in the simplifying of dress has already been noted; as also has the fact that the French revolutionaries wore these simple fashions in the belief that they were essentially English. It is odd to find that the Reaction in France, which had established itself in power by 1795 (or only two years after the guillotining of Queen Marie Antoinette), restored the two-flapped hat—the "lunette," not only for evening but for day wear also; and with the establishment of the Napoleonic family in power, the top-hat was virtually abolished in France.

"Round" hat, 18th cent.

Napoleon, his brothers and all his generals, continued to wear the headgear of the 18th century, and, for formal occasions, the long, collarless coat, heavily embroidered, the knee breeches and silk stockings were worn, where, in England the mode was completely abandoned. The French police, indeed, continued to wear the cocked hat until after the Second Republic; and it is only since the First World War that French generals and admirals have given up the feathered bicorne so strangely reminiscent of the 18th century. British Governors, Governors-General and other functionaries still wear the "fore-and-aft" bicorne with full dress.

Emperor of Haiti, 1808

The most striking change in fashion came with the adoption, by women, of small hats, no more than caps, and the shortening of their hair that the wearing of such simple headgear demanded. The carrying of the European conflict to Egypt, and the interest in the ancient Eygptian civilization that the finding of the Rosetta Stone aroused, introduced both "Egyptian" and "Turkish" fashions (Egypt then being a fief of the Turkish Sultan). Once again the Turban came back into women's fashions, and it was to continue in use until about 1840, when it was supplanted by the poke-bonnet, worn, until, say, 1930, by old women of all classes below the very top, and now retained as a ritual head-dress, by Salvation Army "lasses."

The origin of the poke-bonnet is similar to that of many other distinctive forms of headgear: it originated in an unconventional mode of wearing a hat already in use. The poke-bonnet, in short, is nothing more than the ancient "flower pot" hat, pushed far back on the crown of the head, the back portion being more and more cut away to allow the hat to take in the back of the neck.

The development of the poke-bonnet from the brimmed hat may be traced, through its successive stages, from about 1814, or, say, the defeat of Napoleon; and, as the hat was pushed farther back on the head, so the brim lost its angle in relation to the crown, as well as being reduced in size. The pushed-back hat had become a true poke-bonnet by about 1830; another ten years and it had acquired a universality

Poke bonnet, c. 1830

comparable with that of the male top-hat.   The brims had
been wide in the reign of William IV, but, with the coming of
Victoria, they got smaller, to produce, more or less, the
Salvation Army poke-bonnet of today.   Not until about 1860
did the poke-bonnet meet a vigorous challenge, and the
challenger was the Pork-pie (original name) or Pill-box—a
hat which caught male, as well as female, fancy; the Army
adopting it, and retaining it, in certain units, until the outbreak of the First World War.   The District Messengers kept
it until the early 1930s, and when the Boys' Brigade were recently asked their opinion on this outmoded form of headgear,
they, like the Lincolnshire Police, voted for its retention.

Etonian cap, c. 1830

It is singular but—apparently—true that the fashion of the
Pork-pie was established by the envious admiration in which
Good Women held Miss Catherine Walters, "Skittles," one
of the most brazen and successful harlots of the mid-Victorian
scene.

Skittles, daughter of a Newcastle collier's captain, was a
fine horsewoman, and all London turned out to see her driving
her splendid matched ponies through the Park.   In a letter to
The Times, a contemporary writer had this to say:

> "The highest ladies in the land enlisted themselves as
> (Skittles's) disciples. . . . If she wore a pork-pie hat, they
> wore pork-pie hats. . . . If she reverted to more feminine
> attire, they reverted to it also."

But, though women did, in fact, revert to "more feminine
attire," the younger women did not revert to the poke-bonnet
that Skittles's pork-pie hat had ousted.   The poke-bonnet was
left to elderly women, the nursing profession and the Salvation
Army.   The fashionable women, after having tried out the
plumed Cavalier hat—especially when riding—found a new
way of wearing the bonnet.   They pushed it forward again,
and cut off the material remaining at the back of the head, so
that it now resembled a pork pie, with some trimming at the
back, and with two ribbons either tied under the chin—which
is a very ancient fashion—or with the ribbons falling down the
back, equally ancient.   Not until the very end of the 1880s—

and then under the influence of the "Aesthetic Movement," did the true hat for women reappear.

Of course, the country folk had always worn the wide-brimmed straw, as well as their version of the bonnet—or hood. This bonnet, made of soft material, was known as a "sun-bonnet," and was worn by town girls as well as by rustic women and female children until the beginning of the First World War.

Here it must be pointed out that until recent times, the "basic" hat forms have been permanently retained in what we may call the "wardrobe" of the countryfolk. Like the countryfolk's dances, the Waltz, the Polka and so on, the countryfolk's hats have been adopted, again and again, by the Upper Crust. Given a slightly new form, these "fashionable" forms have descended to the level of the countryfolk, to be rescued, at some later date, by the fashionable. It is for this reason that we find the Commander-in-Chief of the English Army in Ireland, in 1581, wearing what can be described only as a Lock's bowler; and bowlers, top-hats, boaters and the rest are constantly appearing Above simply because they are permanently in use Below.

Mention of the "sun-bonnet" reminds us that, until the First World War, seasonal changes were clearly marked in Britain by the type of headgear that men wore. When one says that, during the 19th century, the top-hat was worn by everyone, this is a remark which applies only to formal dress in an age of elaborate social etiquette.

There were some pretty hot summers during the 19th century, and if the men stuck to formal clothing in Town, when "paying calls," they changed into summer clothing when no longer under the strict sartorial discipline of city convention. If, as Messrs Laver and Cunnington claim, the Victorian men did not leave off underclothes or even waistcoat, whatever the weather, they did leave off their tall hats in favour of light-coloured felt "boaters" or wide-brimmed straw hats—what the British call "Panamas," and the Americans (I am told) "Planters'." The class who stuck it out longest in the sun, wearing top-hats, were the cricketers, and by the 1860s, the

Cricketers' cap, c. 1820

11—H.H.

cricketing top-hat had been replaced by the peakless soft, round cap.

Perhaps it was because of their fidelity to the incredibly unsuitable high beaver or plush top-hat that the custom of giving hats to cricketers originated.

In that most interesting book, *They Made Cricket*, by G. D. Martineau, I found this passage, that I quote here with acknowledgments to the author and to his publishers, The Museum Press:

"Heathfield Harman Stephenson (uncle of S. M. Read) was born in 1833—a good inside batsman, an excellent wicket-keeper, and a fast-medium round-arm bowler of terrific off-breaks.

He had been playing for Surrey since 1853, and for the Players since 1857; he had also visited America with Parr's team in 1859. Stephenson provides us with the earliest example of a hat being given for the taking of three wickets in three successive balls.

This occurred when he was playing for the All England XI against Twenty-two of Hallam and Staveley in 1858. As he had performed this feat twice previously in the same season, without apparently receiving any such reward, it is possible that the custom dates from then."

This, then, appears to be the origin of the well-known phrase, a "hat trick," no longer applied specifically to a cricketing feat, but meaning three separate happenings of the same nature.

Panama, c. 1835

But to go back to summer clothing of the last century: men wore light felt hats and Panamas, and, as the century wore on, the boater, worn in England until 1914 and still worn in America, was introduced. This, apparently, originated in the Bedfordshire town of Luton, and was distinguished by a certain form of manufacture: straw being plaited, and then coiled to form a "shape," which was then moulded into the "boater" form.

The boater was not confined to men: schoolboys wore it, and so did clergymen, though the boater of the clergy was either black or "pepper and salt," a colour which also distinguished the boater worn by certain schools. I recall the "pepper and salt" boaters of the boys of Margate College.

Boaters were popular with women and girls at the end of the 19th century, but, as they were adopted for orphanages, the boaters were given up by the socially self-conscious.

Straw boater, c. 1885

The great Fashion Influence of the 19th century is, without doubt, George IV.

George was a fashion-dictator of imagination and daring, and his influence is with us today. When one overhears American visitors remarking upon the archaic dress of the Life Guards or Horse Guards, one must remember that it was George IV who put the Guards, and practically every other regiment, into dresses which were archaic even in his day. It is curious to reflect that the Napoleonic Wars, which were fought, though with the old weapons and the old tactics against the background of an Industrial Revolution well into its stride, saw the reintroduction of such outmoded military equipment as body armour and sabre-taches, and a host of smaller items of no use whatever even in the early 19th century.

It is too long here to state that arguments for linking all this Romantic costuming of the soldiery with the Gothic novel, and for linking both with a subconscious revolt against the Industrial Revolution (not only Blake saw the mills as "dark" and "Satanic"), but it must be noted that, right up to the French Revolution, and the consequent war with France, the trend of military uniform had been towards simplication, as well as to uniformity.

The irruption of the French revolutionary armies into almost every European country had brought strange and exciting uniforms into the common experience of many of the combatants. The Hungarian and Polish cavalry, with their outlandish headgear and their bizarre uniforms, all silk cord and fur, excited the romantic admiration of friends and enemies alike. Both sides could hardly wait to get into their own equivalent of these colourful uniforms.

Glamorgan Militia, 1778

In 1811, the French had adopted the Polish uniform, with

its distinctive square-topped cap, for their *Chevaux Légers*[1]; but the Brunswick cavalry had adopted it two years before; and in 1813, the Saxon Uhlans, still with the Polish uniform, had been formed.

The British Army adopted the Lancer uniform in 1815, and though the square-topped helmet was not worn, the lances flashed in Mesopotamia as late as 1917. Officers even wore the baggy Cossack trousers.

Peace, in 1815, brought further exotic fashions into the British Army. The bearskin of the Guards was altered to the type worn by Napoleon's Old Guard; and when the Prince Regent became King in 1820, he introduced, not only cuirass and backplate for the Household Brigade, but steel helmets with a huge bearskin crest, so vast that only with difficulty could the men keep themselves upright in the saddle when a high wind was blowing. The late King George VI wished to reintroduce this admittedly very handsome helmet for the Household Brigade; but experiments with soldier "models" soon proved that they were quite unsuitable.

1st Life Guards, 1829

Though the bearskin crests were taken off the steel helmets, and a spike added, from which a horsehair switch falls, it should be observed that the helmet of today is of the same pattern as that introduced by George IV. It is often stated that the spiked "policeman's" helmet, introduced for the British line Regiments after 1870, was adopted because of "Queen Victoria's liking for the Germans." There is no truth in this: the shape of the line regiments' dome-topped helmets is identical with that of the Household Brigade's steel helmets. The only difference is that the line regiments' helmets were faced with cloth.

The bearskin is still worn, of course, but it has changed its shape slightly during the past century and a half. Originally it was higher, with a pronounced forward curve, and though the officers' bearskins are more forward-curving than the men's, both are more "bulgy" than they were in 1815.

---

[1] Later in the century, the Chevaux Légers were given the *talpack*, the brimless astrakhan shako worn by the Turkish Janissaries in the Middle Ages. This was worn with full dress by certain British calvary regiments.

The same firm, by the way, has made the cane-frames for the bearskins since the Crimean War, and this firm, G. W. Scott & Sons Ltd, was founded in 1661, when William Scott, an apprentice basket-maker in the City of London, was admitted to the Basket Maker's Company.

Bethnal Green volunteer's cap, 1799

Two men turn out twenty to thirty cane frames a week, when War Office contracts, which vary in size, are being carried out. Each frame cost from 16s. to 17s. each, is made entirely by hand, and is measured by eye, and not by the use of a hatter's block. Officers' frames are two to three inches higher than those of the rankers.

The fact that the Prince Regent encouraged the adoption of splendid uniforms, and the system of "proprietary" colonelcy which made it possible for colonels to put their men into such uniforms as their wayward fancy could devise, yet introduced a richness into British Army uniform which would not have come about without the wars with France which took our men to the Continent.

The pill-box has already been mentioned; but it was as popular in the Army as with the women. It came, as so many fashions have come, from "off-duty" wear invading the realm of the formal.

Infantry, undress cap, c. 1816

It was never "full dress," but, from being a fatigue cap, it was promoted to "undress" and "walking out," and, decorated with braiding, in a manner reminiscent of the civilian smoking-cap still worn less than forty years ago, and it was *the* soldier's walking-out cap until 1914. A special style of hair-dressing, the "quiff," was developed to accompany the tilted-to-one-side pill-box. We have already seen that District Messengers and the Boys' Brigade adopted this essentially military headgear, and retained it long after it had been abolished in the Army. The officers wore it too, but, after a time added a straight-down peak, and wore it straight, not at an angle. And no officer sported a "quiff."

Turning back to the civilians; under the sovereign rule of the Top-hat, there were rebels right from the beginning. Several years before Keir Hardie "scandalized" the House of Commons by turning up in a "cloth cap" (actually, it was a

The "Deerstalker," from c. 1875

"Sherlock Holmes" deerstalker, and a perfectly proper hat for travelling), *The Illustrated London News*, of February 23rd, 1861, had this to say about a more tolerated Member: "Mr Hubbard . . . wears a "wide-awake" hat, which is a novelty in the House." The pictures of the time show that Mr Hubbard was not the only rebel against the total tyranny of the Top-hat, and these rebels included many people far beyond the arty circles of the Pre-Raphaelites. Before the end of the century, the rebels had driven two wide breaches into the bastion of Top-Hattery: that of the Wide-awake or Bowler, and that of the Soft-hat, which had to be "rescued" from its "artistic" form of "Trilby" by being given a form midway between the formality of the hard hat and the informality of the Trilby. Only when the Homburg—"sanctioned" by the great frequenter of Homburg itself, Edward, Prince of Wales—gained, first, near-equality with the Top-hat, and then a lead over it, did the Homburg retire gracefully before the Soft Felt, or Trilby, whose dominance the Homburg had affected. With their stronger traditional sense, the Americans have remained faithful to the Homburg, which may be seen on the heads of older Americans, in what by the turn of the century was to remain its standard form: pearl-grey felt, black hat-band, whitish-grey Petersham edging to the symmetrically curving brim.

A word about colour; brown was for long a "taboo" colour: "Good enough for bookies, but not for gentlemen." Lady Troubridge, in her book on Etiquette, solemnly advises the newcomer into polite usage: "Never wear brown boots in London, unless you wish to earn the sneer of the footman." A brown hat would have curled the lip of Jeames as effectively.

When Michael Arlen's *Green Hat* was published in 1924, a passage from George Jean Nathan's review went something like this: "What's all this fuss over a green hat . . . ? Come to that, I wear a green hat myself."

A *green* hat—for a *man*! In those days, only the most daring would think of wearing a soft hat in anything but grey: brown, as a colour, was just creeping in for soft hats—the word "trilby" (with a lower-case "t") had already become

Bowler, late Victorian

what has since been called, "Non-U." Incidentally, the phrase, "soft felt," has never been used save by hatters.

The 19th century saw the triumph of one hat material for men's hats. At the beginning of the century, the *Penny Cyclopaedia* could say: "There are three descriptions or qualities of hats made of wool, viz., beaver-hats, plate-hats and felt-hats." The *Cyclopaedia* added: "Silk-hats are composed of a form made of chip or of felt, and covered with woven silk plush or shag." "When the outer batt is considerably finer than the inner one, the retailers term it a 'plated hat'."

The modern top hat

But, at the end, the only tall hat was a "silk" one, and the triumph of felt, in its pure form (either as Trilby, Homburg or Bowler) was assured. Curiously enough, there was, and still is, an actual silk hat: that is, made of silk poplin. This is the so-called "crush hat," reputedly the invention of a French hatter named Gibus, whose name the hat long bore. It was invented in the days when men did not leave their hats in the "cloak room," but only their cloaks: they took their hats into the theatre with them.

This collapsible hat was, in reality, a *chapeau bras*, and the last to be invented, though the older *chapeau bras* continued to be carried as a part of Court dress until that ritual garb was abolished just before the last war.

To revert to the point that the 19th century saw the triumph of felt, I quote here a letter written to the author by Mr J. M. McNulty, Secretary of the British Felt Hat Manufacturers' Federation. Mr McNulty's letter is given in full, as surely not since the day when St Crispin invented felt by accident has the nature and manufacture of felt been more fully or more clearly explained.

Mr McNulty writes:

"The Felt Hat Industry, although not one of the largest industries in the country is, nevertheless, a very important one, and has, on many occasions, been called the 'Crown' trade of the country.

"For instance, how many people know that there are *two*

distinctive kinds of felt . . . the one made from wool of sheep . . . (the wool felt) . . . and the other made from the fur of the rabbit . . . (the fur felt) in which sometimes other fur fibres from the hare, the beaver and the nutria, may be added.

"Then how many people know that their hat, size 6⅞ths, shall we say, starts off in the initial process as a huge cone-shaped form, some 24 inches high and measuring some 30 inches across its base (looking for all the world like an outsize of the circus clown's hat we all know so well). And finally, how many realize that to make a hat, whether of fur or wool, there may be up to as many as fifty different and separate processes involved before the finished hat, be it for a lady or a man, ultimately finds its way on to the hat-stand of the milliner or retailer! At the expense of repeating them, let us just make sure of those questions. We now know that my hat, or your hat, in the first stage of manufacture was a large mass of animal fibres, fur or wool, loosely placed together usually in the form of a cone. This cone by a series of skilled operations is transformed and shrunk into the tight uniform material we know and recognize as felt, and from which it is difficult to pick out the individual fibres.

"Sugar loaf" cap, English, 11th cent.

"With that out of the way we can now look in greater detail at our raw materials and processes and see what contributions science has made, and can make, to what every practical hatter proudly calls 'the art and mystery of hat making.'

"It is truly surprising to know that the foundation of the felt hat is either the rabbit or the sheep. The better grade hats are made from the fur of the rabbit, and the lower quality hats from the wool of the sheep.

"The manipulation of these two raw materials is somewhat different in the earlier stages of the manufacture of the hat.

"With regard to the fur hat, the basic material is rabbit or hare skins, which are prepared by the hatters' furriers. This preparation consist of 'Carotting'—which is the operation of treating the fur with a solution of nitrate of mercury, whereby the felting properties are considerably increased and so called because the tips of the fur become a reddish yellow in colour. After this process the skin is passed to the cutting machine which separates the fur from the pelt. Under the action of the cutting-knives the skin is shredded off and the fur so freed is used by the hat manufacturer. Only the back of the fur is used in making hats of good quality and blending of the fur is an art. Considerable knowledge and skill are necessary in this department.

"The fur then requires cleaning or 'blowing,' by which process the kemps (coarse hairs) which will not felt, and dags (small pieces of pelt) are extracted from the fur. This operation is carred out in a long casing of wood and glass provided with a series of compartments enclosed in fine wire netting through which passes a travelling endless apron carrying the fur. A current of air, set up by the rotation of the pickers, lifts the fur, separates it and tosses it into the air. The heavier hairs and dust fall into a space between the endless apron and picker, whilst the finer fur is carried on further and finally leaves the machine ready for making into hats. The blown fur is weighed in sufficient quantity for a hat and placed on a travelling apron at the upper part of the forming machine. By means of a current of air this machine separates the mass of fur and allows it to fall in a fine state on a large perforated copper cone which is enclosed in a glass chamber. The fur carried down from the top of the chamber is drawn on to the cone uniformly over the surface by suction while the cone is revolving. When all the fur for one hat has been blown on to the cone it is sprayed with hot water and the 'Form,' as it is then called, is taken from the cone.

"The average size of a hat form of 'Dunce's Cap' before shrinking is, as stated, about 24 inches high by 30 inches wide. The first process of felting is termed 'Hardening.' This operation consists of rolling three or more hat forms in cloth until the felting or 'matting' process begins and then the hoods pass on to planking.

"Reverting to the wool hat, the raw material of which is, of course, the wool from the sheep; this, of course, is very uncouth, and needs to be scoured in hot water and purified in chemicals. The scouring process, which takes place after the wool has been blended, consists of the wool being agitated backwards and forwards by mechanical raikes in a hot bath, and afterwards it is chemically treated so that the vegetable matter—the burrs and seeds which are entangled in it—may be removed.   For light colours, the wool undergoes a further chemical process to remove all traces of tar or paint with which the sheep were branded by the farmer.   By carding, the wool, which is now a much more polite and presentable substance, is straightened out.   The operation is common to all wool manufacturers, and it is at the close of it that the differentiations of felt are seen to begin.   The first of these processes which are special to hat felting is the process known as wool-forming. At what we may call the back door of the carding machine is a wooden cone, and this cone is of the shape that would be produced by the joining together at their base of two hats such as we see the pierrots wear.   This cone receives the wool as it leaves the carding machine.   Revolving and oscillating very slowly, like a top that is running down, the cone entwines itself in wool, and when the oscillating operation is complete and the cocoon of wool has been cut in two at the thickest part we have two hat shapes, flimsy and misty things indeed, but of just sufficient cohesion to take the toughening process of which felting properly consists.   The shapes seem at this stage extravagantly large, but in felting the size of the material will dwindle while its strength grows.

"We have now arrived at the process of wool-hardening, which is very similar to the hardening process as explained in regard to the fur form.

"From this stage, up to the completed hat, the fur and the wool form undergo very similar processes, and both the product of the rabbit and that of the sheep can be taken together.

"Planking, therefore, is the next process, and this consists of shrinking the 'form' or 'hood' to a suitable tightness by a method of rolling under pressure.   The hood must be kept as hot as possible by the application of boiling water to which sulphuric acid has been added to help the shrinking.   The form becomes gradually smaller and, when the shrinking (felting) is completed, the hood will measure about 10½ inches high by 15½ inches wide and is tough enough to stand hard wear. After drying, the hood is placed on a swiftly revolving cone-shaped block and shaved with sand-paper to remove any loose, overlong or untidy hair.

"The dyeing of soft felt hats may be done at several different stages of manufacture. For coloured fur hats the fur can be dyed before the hat is formed, or the hoods may be dyed when half planked and the shrinking completed later. The dyeing of the soft hat, made of wool, is usually done before the final process of planking. Hard hats, both of fur and wool, are dyed after stiffening. During the dyeing process the hoods may be placed in an open kettle where they are stirred by hand with long wooden poles, or in closed revolving cylinders which dip into the dye at each revolution. Again pressure dyeing may be used where colour is forced through the felt body.

"For soft hats the stiffening or 'proofing' is done with a solution of shellac dissolved in hot water and borax which is applied to the felt between two rollers, one on the inside and the other on the outside of the hood, and then submitted to steam to drive it into the felt. Hard felt hats are stiffened with shellac dissolved in methylated spirit.

"The dyed and proofed hood is now stretched or shaped by machine and from this stage gradually loses its cone shape and becomes the shape of hat desired. After being stretched the hats are 'blocked' to the specific shape and size required by being steamed and pulled on to a wood block and allowed to cool.

"The blocked hat, after drying, is pressed in an iron dish of the same size and shape, and is then ready for finishing. This operation consists of hand or machine rubbing of the hats with very fine sand-paper until the correct smoothness or finish is obtained.

"The hat is now ready for brim shaping. The brims are deftly manipulated by skilled operatives. The brims of stiff hats may be curled by hand, or an iron matrice made the same width, style and set as the desired shape, which is then carefully pared prior to trimming. Soft hats are curled first on a machine and the final style is given by flanging the hat on a wooden frame of the required shape, the pressure being supplied by heated sandbags.

"The hat is now ready for trimming, i.e., the final process. Linings are prepared separately and fastened in, the bindings or ribbons sown on the brim edge, leathers (previously printed and sewn round the top) cut to the correct length and fitted in the hats, and bands with bows sewn round the crown of the hat.

"Thus it may be said with some degree of truth that the conjurer's trick of producing a rabbit from a hat has been reversed by the hatmaker, who can, before your eyes, produce a hat from a rabbit or a sheep!

"Although it may have been noticed that the above processes seem to apply to men's hats only, with very small variations ladies' felt hats undergo the same treatment, though the variations and original characteristics demanded by the ladies are the greatest difficulties here. Generally speaking, men's hats are made, more or less, uniform in style and character, but in ladies' hats, the less uniformity there is the greater is the appeal to the purchaser.

"The manufacture of felt hats is centred to a large degree in some half dozen towns round Manchester, although wool hats are also produced in Warwickshire. In these districts the hats are made by the manufacturers throughout, as explained previously, and so the claim to be hat manufacturers is well defined. There are other districts in Great Britain where the hat is completed in its latter stages only. These makers buy the bodies or hoods in the dyed stage, and then just complete the finishing processes outlined above.

"Manufacturing up to the hood or 'halfway' stage is today a much increased trade due to a large extent to the demands of the Ladies' Milliner whose job it is to continually create new and appealing hats to the very individualistic and everchanging tastes of the consumer. Of this Hood Trade a large proportion is done by the makers centred around the Luton area."

Flat-topped, large-brimmed

It was in 1856 that an official uniform was devised for the Royal Navy sailor. It seems strange that the Senior Service should have had to wait until the middle of the 19th century to be awarded a uniform dress. But the sea's influence was felt long before the sailor got an official dress: and boaters for the more-or-less adults and "real" sailors' hats for the children were the fashion for many years both before and after the official naval uniform was decreed in 1856. The first "uniform" hat of the sailor was a wide-brimmed straw, with the brim turned up all the way round; not until the third quarter of the century did he get his round, peakless cap, softer than it is today, and with a slightly wider top. The straw hat was retained, but in light-coloured straw, trimmed with blue Petersham ribbon, and if the top-hat was universally worn by male adults, the straw sailor's hat was universally worn by children of all classes.

We have talked about the usurpation, by the Homburg, of the Top-hat's pre-eminent position: it seems that the adoption of the Homburg by women in the 1890s may have had something to do with its being popularized. The New Woman celebrated her freedom—a freedom given to her, by the way, through the Bicycle and not through the Law—in adopting the most masculine of clothes. She wore divided shirts (the petticoat-breeches fashionable in the 1660s and still worn by sailors until about 1830), and bloomers; but even when she did not wear these, she went in for tweeds of a masculine cut and adorned her head with a man's Homburg, to which she added, in some sort of deference to her sex, half a stuffed grouse.

King Edward VII wearing Homburg, c. 1900

The working woman, in the towns, wore straw hats as a girl; then black, usually velvet, "boaters" as a young woman, and some sort of mannish hat or cap as a middle-aged woman. When she had to admit that age had overtaken her, she went into a jet-trimmed black bonnet.

In London though, the young girls wore straw hats, but the adult women wore wide-brimmed cavalier hats, trimmed with "fevvers": on "Sunday and holiday," but not to work.

Her man wore either a high-crowned bowler, in whitish-grey, or a cap with the cloth top panelled out in star-form. Elderly "Cockney" women wore a man's hat, kept perfectly flat, and pinned to the screwed-down hair by means of hat pins.

It is a truth that a century does not really end until twenty years or so of the following century have passed; and up to about 1920, the customs of the 19th century lingered on among the simpler folk.

Man's cap, c. 1905

We have seen how the two-peaked shako of the postman lingered on until 1932, but the specialized trades' headgear did not pass until some time between 1920 and 1930. The coal-man's hat, with its round close-fitting crown, and huge flap hanging down the back; the printer's and carpenter's hand-made square brown-paper cap (the Carpenter in *Alice* is wearing one), the stocking cap of the brewer: all these and many others lingered on almost until the beginning of the last war.

Today, only the boater of the fishmonger and butcher remains as a trade head-dress, apart from such self-conscious hats as those of town criers and beadles.

Chapter Thirteen

FROM VICTORIA TO THE WELFARE STATE

THE first 'mechanical clarence' (as Scotland Yard calls a taxi) was licensed in 1897; and buses and motor cars and tube-trains were to abolish frock-coats and top-hats. When the Guards attended the 1913 manœuvres in khaki, the change into a drab uniform merely reflected the establishment of a universal drabness. In the first chapter of this book, I talked about the valiantly romantic-reactionary characters who tried to infuse some poetry into their fearful peaked caps by turning them into Gorblimeys.

The Gorblimeys have gone: only the telegram boys take liberties with their peaked caps. For all the others wear the same sort of peaked cap.

There was this about the age of the Hat: everyone wore it, and wore it all the time. There is a picture of Queen Victoria taking breakfast under the trees of Osborne: all are wearing hats, even the young Princes. There is a picture of a fashionable crowd at the Royal Academy—all wear hats.

And we seem to be taking to hats again. The First World War put everyone into a hat—even women bus-conductors, munition-workers, postwomen, WAACs—but there was a noticeable falling off in hat-wearing after that first global conflict, as the newspapers called it. The Second World War seems to have done what the first failed to do: put us back among the Hatted again.

This trend towards hatlessness was noticed by that astute observer of human behaviour, the late Lord Northcliffe, and he made a gallant effort to bring back, if not the hat, then at least a lively interest in it.

On September 1st, 1920, Lord Northcliffe's *Daily Mail* carried an article, headed (in the then bold 24-point type):

MEN'S DOWDY HATS

The article went on to explain that the *Daily Mail* was offering a prize of £100 for a new hat.

It quoted the famous artist, Mr C. R. W. Nevinson, as saying:

"The hard felt hat of today is typical of the modern man. It is neither beautiful nor useful. The top-hat is a survival of the old highwayman's hat, and it is rather more artistic, but no one can say it is pleasant to wear.

"If anyone proposes to design a new type of hat for men, I should advise them to think only of making it useful. If it is strictly utilitarian, it will probably be artistic also, but if they think of making it beautiful, it will probably be both inconvenient and ugly.

"The ideal hat must be waterproof, warm and easy to take on and off. A far greater variety of colours for men's hats might be employed than at present."

Mr Nevinson recommended a "type of tam-o'-shanter like that worn by the students of Paris." Mr Nevinson found such a cap both "becoming and beautiful."

Lord Arthur Hill and numerous other notables were roped in by Lord Northcliffe to declare themselves in favour of a new hat.

Each day, for seven weeks, the *Daily Mail* printed a selection of readers' suggestions—drawings—which ran the gamut of hattery (we thought it mad-hattery) from the fez of Sardanapalus to a square-topped silk-hat, like a Lancer's helmet with a curly brim.

On October 20th, 1920, the newspaper carried this head:

THE "DAILY MAIL"

SANDRINGHAM HAT

Forty thousand suggestions had been sent in, but the prize of £100 had been won by a young Civil Servant, Mr A. O. Hopkins, of New Cross, London. The article told the *Mail*'s readers that Sir William Orpen had consented to wear the Sandringham, and it described how the hatters, had worked overtime to produce the hat.

". . . To make the blocks for the new hat has been a matter of working against time, but so keen were the blockmakers . . . to do their part that they worked on Sunday last."

The hat, though "modelled" by the handsome youngish *jeune premier*, Mr Owen Nares, was disappointing.

"Good God!" said my father, when he saw it. "What's new about that flat-topped billycock? Why, dammit, King George wears one—*has* done, for years."

All the same, the attempt to make a new hat was a commendable one; and, four years later, as I recall, there was another attempt to smarten up our heads—though this attempt was a spontaneous one, and not "inspired" to increase a newspaper's circulation. This attempt was on the part of a number of young men, who abandoned "lounge suits" and "trilbies," and adopted the almost outmoded morning-coat and "white topper." It was, I recall, the year of the Rodeo, and the last year when it was still "done" for young men to wear spats.

The curious thing is that Mr Nevinson's desire to see the "tam-o'-shanter of the Paris art-student" adopted was granted—though after Nevinson, a most gifted artist and a charming man, had died. Whoever it is in the British Army who regulates sartorial matters put the soldiery into "tammies" —"Balmorals," they were called.

Sloppy things, they would not have pleased Nevinson, whose artist's eye, once he had moved (about 1915) from chocolate-box art, had an angular quality.

Yet, for all the changes, the hat is back—and it has come back to its beginning. From 1900 onwards, women's hats got bigger and bigger; more and more adorned with feathers. From 1914 onwards, they got smaller and smaller, until the nadir of "economy" was reached with the cloche. After that, the hats got a little bigger, but never to the "cartwheel" magnitude of 1911.

As for men, they abandoned the top-hat, and took to the Homburg; abandoning the Homburg, they adopted, almost universally, the "trilby," or "soft felt." Then, from about 1940, the bowler made a come back; though a serious challenger was the black Homburg, the "Anthony Eden," so eagerly taken up by Sir Anthony's political rivals, who, however, failed to wear it with Eden's customary elegance. Unfortunately, the black Homburg is attractive only when new, and when worn by a naturally elegant man.

Round, small-brimmed type, with dented crown

The last war saw many a new hat—that is to say, many an old hat revived for modern use. The female naval clerks were given the three-cornered hat, both in Britain and in America; the female policemen were given, first the flat-topped, peaked cap, and afterwards a shako. The female Air Force clerks were given a shako, with a rounded top: a hat of most unbecoming design. Only by the Army's female strong-arm squads is the man's flat-topped peaked cap retained.

The children are now reverting to the peakless "skull cap." For that which is, is that which hath been, and there is no new thing under the sun.

SOURCE MATERIAL

It gives me pleasure to acknowledge my deep indebtedness to the following works of history, art, costume and social science, as well as standard reference-books, that I have consulted, though, in making my acknowledgments, I must necessarily leave out all but the principal aids to my research.

However, mentioned or not, the editors and authors of all the works that I have consulted—living or dead—are here tendered my grateful thanks.

Aberdare, Lord. *The Story of Tennis.*
Allen, Agnes. *The Story of Clothes.*
Arnott Hamilton, J. *Byzantine Architecture and Decoration.*
Ashton, John. *Old Times: A Picture of Social Life at the End of the 18th Century.*
Bayle-Mouillard, E. F. C. *Manuel des Dames* (1827).
Beyerle, Guillaume. *Costumes du Moyen Age Chrétien.*
Bonnard, Camille. *Costumes Historiques des XIIIe, XIVe et XVe Siècles.*
Bradley, Carolyn G. *A History of World Costume.*
Brooke, Iris. *English Costume of the Early Middle Ages, the 10th to the 15th Centuries.*
　　English Costume of the Later Middle Ages, the 14th and 15th Centuries.
　　English Costume in the Age of Elizabeth, the 16th Century.
Brooke, Iris, and Laver, James. *English Costume of the Seventeenth Century.*
　　English Costume of the Nineteenth Century.
Calthrop, Dion Clayton. *English Costume.*
　　English Dress from Victoria to George V.
Carman, W. Y. *British Military Uniforms, from Contemporary Pictures—Henry VII to the Present Day.*
Challanul, Augustin. *Histoire de Costume en France.*
Costume, Nineteenth Century. Victoria & Albert Museum, London.
Cunnington, C. Willet & Phillis. *Handbook of English Mediaeval Costume.*
　　Handbook of English Costume in the Sixteenth Century.
　　Handbook of English Costume in the Seventeenth Century.
　　Handbook of English Costume in the Eighteenth Century.
　　Handbook of English Costume in the Nineteenth Century.

Cunnington, C. Willet & Phillis & Charles Beard. *A Dictionary of English Costume, 900–1900.*

Dergny, Dieudonné. *Usages, Costumes et Croyances, ou Livre des Choses Curieuses.*

Dighton, Robert. *English Heads and Coiffures* (1778).

Dress, The Art of; or a Guide to the Toilette; with Directions for adapting the various Parts of the Female Costume to the Complexion or Figure. Anon. London: 1839.

Edwards, Major T. J. *Military Customs.*
  Standards, Guidons and Colours of the Commonwealth Forces.

Evans, Joan. *Dress in Mediaeval France.*
  A History of Jewellery.

Fawcett, Frank Burlington. *Court Ceremonial and Book of the Court.*

Franklin, A. F. A. *La vie privée d'autrefois; arts et métiers, modes, mœurs, usages des Parisiens du XII. au XVIII. siècle.*

Genin, J. N. *An Illustrated History of the Hat* (1848).

Giafferi, P. L. V., Marquis di. *Histoire du Costume Feminin Français.*
  Les Modes du Moyen Age, 1037–1461.
  Histoire du Costume Masculin Français.

Goater, A. C. *A Short Treatise on Headwear, Ancient and Modern* (1885).

Grand-Carteret, John. *Les Elégances de la Toilette: Robes, Chapeaux, Coiffures de Style, 1780–1825.*

Gründ et Maquet. *Français de l'Epoque Carlovingienne à la Renaissance.*

Harvey, John. *Gothic England.*

Heard, Gerald. *Narcissus, an Anatomy of Clothes.*

Heath, William. *Foreign Military Costume* (1823).
  British Military Costume (1824).
  Military Costume of the British Cavalry (1823).

Hill, Georgiana. *A History of English Dress, from the Saxon Period to the Present Day.*

Hope, Thomas. *Costume of the Ancients.*

Houston, Mary G. *Ancient Greek, Roman and Byzantine Costume.*
  Mediaeval Costume in England and France: the Thirteenth, Fourteenth and Fifteenth Centuries.

Hut, Der; Ein kulturhistorisches Essay, mit benutzung einer amerikanischen Arbeit (1869).

Kelly, Francis M., and Schwabe, Rudolph. *Historic Costume, 1490–1790.*

Lacroix, P. *Manners, Customs and Dress during the Middle Ages and during the Renascence Period.*

Laver, James. *Costume of the Western World, 1485–1588.*
> British Military Uniforms.
> Taste and Fashion.
Lawson, Cecil C. P. *A History of the Uniforms of the British Army.*
Lethaby, W. R. *Medieval Art.*
Luton Public Museum. *The Romance of the Straw Hat.*
Manchester, Herbert. *Romance of Men's Hats.*
Margerand, L. *Les Coiffures de l'Armée Française, 1909–1929.*
Martineau, G. D. *They Made Cricket.*
Melton, Henry. *Hints on Hats adapted to the Needs of the People* (1865).
Norris, Herbert. *Costume and Fashion.* (Volume 6–19th century is jointly by Herbert Norris and Oswald Curtis).
Nott, J. C., and Gliddon, G. R. *Types of Mankind* (1854).
Oxford History of English Art, The.
Parducci, Amos. *Costumi, Ornati, Studi sugli Insegnamenti di Cortigiania Medievali.*
Patty, V. C. *Hats and How to Make Them.*
Picken, May Brooks. *The Fashion Dictionary of Fabrics, Sewing and Dress, as expressed in the Language of Fashion.*
Penny Cyclopaedia, 1838.
Planché, Sir James Robinson. *A Cyclopaedia of Costume, or Dictionary of Dress.*
> *History of British Costume, from the Earliest Period to the Close of the 18th Century.*
Power, Eileen. *Mediaeval People.*
Pugin, Augustus. *A Glossary of Ecclesiastical Costume.*
Quennell, M. C. & C. H. B. *A History of Everyday Things in England.*
Raynham, F. G., and Calvert, W. S. G. *Post Office Uniforms.*
Rosenthal, Doris. *Pertaining to Costume.*
Sala, George Augustus. *The Hats of Humanity, Historically, Humorously and Authentically Considered.*
Shaw, Henry. *Dresses and Decoration of the Middle Ages.*
Spon's Encyclopaedia of the Industrial Arts, 1879.
Timidior, O. *Der Hut und seine Geschicht.*
Wadleigh, R. H. *Head gear antique and modern.*
Wilcox, R. Turner. *The Mode in Hats and Headdress.*
Woolley, E. M. *A century of hats and the hats of the century.*
Young, Agnes Brooks. *Recurring Cycles of Fashion, 1760–1937.*

INDEX

INDEX

Great
Parliamentary Occasions

by ENOCH POWELL
M.B.E., M.P., M.A.

These descriptions of famous occasions in Parliament from the fourteenth to the twentieth century provide authentic glimpses of the past, enlivened and enriched by the observations of eye-witnesses and contemporaries. Many, though not all, of the scenes here recreated illustrate the assertion of some liberty. Maybe a privilege of Parliament was under assault, or the freedom of the individual or, as in the case of the Reform Bill of 1831, claims asserted from outside against Parliament itself.

Clearly revealed in these fascinating pages is the way in which Parliament's behaviour has been affected through the centuries by the setting in which it meets, and the unchanging instinct of its Members for observing traditional procedures. Examples of this are to be seen in the author's descriptions of the emergence of the Speaker in 1376, the deposition of Richard II, the attempt by Charles I to arrest the Five Members, the Lords' division on Habeas Corpus, Pitt's speech against the Slave Trade, and, in more recent times, the debate on the Prayer Book.

Mr. Enoch Powell, himself an eminent parliamentarian, concludes his preface to this book with the words: "Anonymous speakers in the Commons of 1376, the characters in the Long Parliament of 1641, the tellers in the Lords in 1679—all have their doubles in Parliament to-day. A study of Parliament is a study of human nature."

Illustrated from photographs and contemporary prints.
Large Crown 8vo. 13s. 6d. net

HERBERT JENKINS LTD., 3 Duke of York Street, London, S.W.1

Princes of Wales

by L. G. PINE

In 1284 Edward I, following his conquest of Wales, created his son Prince of Wales to appease Welsh sentiment. From that time on the title has been in the possession of the male heir to the throne when that heir has been the Sovereign's eldest surviving son, but only when the Sovereign has willed so to create him.

In this deeply interesting book we follow the stories of Plantagenet, Lancastrian, Yorkist, Tudor, Stuart and Hanoverian Princes of Wales until we come to Edward VII—sixty years Prince of Wales—George V, Edward VIII and now Prince Charles. The author describes the ceremony of the Investiture in all its significance and shows how the education and training of the Princes of Wales have varied down the centuries with the particular needs and circumstances of the times. To-day, as in mediaeval days, the training is thorough and intensive, which has not always been the case, particularly under the Hanoverian kings.

Frequently one hears the questions asked:—is the office of Prince of Wales one of state importance and responsibility, or only of ceremony? Is the Prince in some sense the deputy of the Sovereign? Is he permitted to read the state papers that are customarily submitted to the Monarch? These and many other questions are answered in this full and detailed picture of this great royal office.

Illustrated from photographs   21s. net

HERBERT JENKINS LTD., 3 Duke of York Street, London, S.W.1